BARRON'S
COMMON CORE SUCCESS
LEARN, REVIEW, APPLY

GRADE 5 ENGLISH LANGUAGE ARTS

what's
your
STORY

Robin Glenn

Consulting Editor

All inquiries should be addressed to:
Barron's Educational Series, Inc.
250 Wireless Boulevard
Hauppauge, NY 11788
www.barronseduc.com

ISBN 978-1-4380-0677-2

Library of Congress Control Number: 2015932520

Date of Manufacture: April 2015
Manufactured by: C&C Offset Printing Co., Ltd, Shenzhen, China

Printed in China

9 8 7 6 5 4 3 2 1

Title page ©Zurijeta/Shutterstock, Page 5 ©Samuel Borges Photography/Shutterstock, Page 6 ©Veronica Louro/Shutterstock, Page 9 ©Paket/Shutterstock, Page 10 ©Monkey Business Images/Shutterstock, Page 12 ©Luciano Mortula/Shutterstock, Page 14 ©Everett Historical/Shutterstock, Page 16 ©Zack Frank/Shutterstock, Page 18 (top) ©Alexey Kamenskiy/Shutterstock, (bottom) ©Merkushev Vasiliy/Shutterstock, Page 20 ©AVAVA/Shutterstock, Page 21 ©Paket/Shutterstock, Page 22 ©American Spirit/Shutterstock, Page 23 ©Victorian Traditions/Shutterstock, Page 27 ©Mike Flippo/Shutterstock, Page 30 ©Jose Gil/Shutterstock, Page 31 ©Everett Historical/Shutterstock, Page 32 ©Sergey Novikovt/Shutterstock, Page 35 ©American Spirit/Shutterstock, Page 36 ©patrimonio designs ltd/Shutterstock, Page 39 ©Jesser/Shutterstock, Page 40 Photo courtesy of the Library of Congress), Page 41 ©Martha Dean/Shutterstock, Page 42 ©Charlesimage/Shutterstock, Page 46 Photo courtesy of the Library of Congress, (bottom) ©catwalker/Shutterstock, Page 50 ©AnnaLotsky/Shutterstock, Page 52 ©Siberia-Video and Photo/Shutterstock, Page 53 ©Scott Rothstein/Shutterstock, Page 54 Photo courtesy of the Library of Congress, Page 58 Photo courtesy of the Library of Congress, Page 64 ©Kovalchuk Oleksandr/Shutterstock, Page 67 ©Corey Smith/Shutterstock, Page 69 ©AVAVA/Shutterstock, Page 71 ©muratart/Shutterstock, Page 72 ©Susan Coons Photography, Page 73 ©Gary C. Tognoni/Shutterstock, Page 74 ©Pal Teravagimov/Shutterstock, Page 75 ©Blakely/Shutterstock, Page 76 ©Corpusimages/Shutterstock, Page 78 ©Dmitry Kaminsky /Shutterstock, Page 79 ©Vtlife/Shutterstock, Page 80 ©Durden Images/Shutterstock, Page 84 ©Andrey Armyagov/Shutterstock, Page 85 ©kaarsten/Shutterstock, Page 86 ©Mitch Crown/Shutterstock, Page 90 ©Rich Caren/Shutterstock, Page 92 ©naluwan/Shutterstock, Page 93 ©parmoht hongtong/Shutterstock, Page 94 ©Matt Jeppson/Shutterstock, Page 97 ©Rich Carey/Shutterstock Page 98 ©Inara Prusakova /Shutterstock, Page 100 ©Wuan/Shutterstock, Page 101 ©Brigid Sturgeon/Shutterstock, Page 103 ©Mr. Lightman/Shutterstock, Page 107 ©Hein Image/Shutterstock, ©Steve Cukrov/Shutterstock, Page 108 ©clearviewstock/Shutterstock, Page 109 ©HARELUYA/Shutterstock, Page 115 ©totallyPic.com/Shutterstock, Page 116 ©Paul Hakimata Photography/Shutterstock, Page 117 ©Paket/Shutterstock, Page 118 ©D.J.McGee /Shutterstock, Page 119 ©Ron and John/Shutterstock, John Henry: The Steel Driving Man, reprinted with permission of S.E.Schlosser, Page 120 Photo courtesy of the Library of Congress, Page 121 ©Sergey Novikovt/Shutterstock, Page 123 Courtesy of the Chesapeake and Ohio Historical Society, Page 124 ©Monkeybusiness/Shutterstock, Pecos Bill reprinted with permission of S.E. Schlosser; Page 125 ©Seita/Shutterstock, Page 128 ©steckfigures/Shutterstock, Page 131 (top) ©Photo Image/Shutterstock, (bottom); Page 133 ©JUCKO/Shutterstock; Page 134 ©Tony Wear/Shutterstock, Page 136 ©Hein Nouwens/Shutterstock, Page 139 ©NguyenLuong Pictures/Shutterstock, Page 140 ©Monkey Business Images/Shutterstock, Page 141 ©Dn Br /Shutterstock, Page 142 ©Jeane09/Shutterstock, Page 144 © Istomina Olena/Shutterstock, Page 146 (top) ©Eric Isselee/Shutterstock, (bottom) ©Konstantin Shevtsov/Shutterstock, Page 148 ©Erni/Shutterstock , Page 149 ©Kopirin/Shutterstock, Page 150 ©Andresr/Shutterstock Page 151 ©tmcphotos/Shutterstock, Page 154 ©YuryZap/Shutterstock ©Slavapolo/Shutterstock Page 155 ©Pinkpueblo/Shutterstock, Page 156 ©Pinkpueblo/Shutterstock, Page 158 ©Soloviova Liudmyla/Shutterstock, Page 159 ©Nordling/Shutterstock, Page 161 ©Sextoacto/Shutterstock, Page 162 (top) ©John L. Absher/Shutterstock, (bottom) ©YANGCHAO/Shutterstock, Page 163 ©Koshevnyk/Shutterstock, Page 166 (top) ©ktak2s/Shutterstock, (bottom) ©catwalker/Shutterstock, Page 169 (top) ©Pink Pueblo/Shutterstock, (bottom) ©Anna Kucherova/Shutterstock, Page 170 ©Carlos Caetano/Shutterstock, "DREAMS" from THE COLLECTED POEMS BY LANGSTON HUGHES by Langston Hughes edited by Arnold Rempersand with Davie Roessel, Associate Editor, © 1994 by the estate of Langston Hughes. Used by permission of Alfred A Knopf, an imprint of the Knopf Doubleday Publishing Group, a division of Random House LLC. All rights reserved., Page 174 ©Jamie Roach/Shutterstock

As of August 2013, forty-six states and the District of Columbia had adopted the Common Core State Standards (CCSS) for English Language Arts (ELA) literacy and mathematics. These standards are geared toward preparing students for college, careers, and competition in the global economy. The adoption of the CCSS represents the first time that schools across the nation have had a common set of expectations for what students should know and be able to do. As with any new program, there are growing pains associated with implementation. Teachers are busy adapting classroom materials to meet the standards, and many parents are confused about what the standards mean for their children. As such, it is a prime opportunity for the creation of a workbook series that provides a clear-cut explanation of the standards coupled with effective lessons and activities tied to those standards.

The foundation of Barron's English Language Arts (ELA) literacy workbook for the fifth grade is based on sound educational practices coupled with parent-friendly explanations of the standards and interesting activities for students that meet those standards. While many other workbook series on the market today offer students practice with individual skills outlined in the CCSS, none seem to do so in a cohesive manner. Our goal was to create an exciting series that mirrors the way teachers actually teach in the classroom. Rather than random workbook pages that present each of the CCSS skills in isolation, our series presents the skills in interesting units of related materials that reinforce each of the standards in a meaningful way. We have included Stop and Think (Review/ Understand/Discover) sections to assist parents/ tutors and students in applying those skills at a higher level. The standards being addressed in each unit are clearly labeled and explained throughout so that parents/tutors have a better grasp of the purpose behind each activity. Additionally, fifth graders will be familiar and comfortable with the manner of presentation and learning as this is what they should be accustomed to in their everyday school experiences. These factors will not only assist students in mastering the skills of the standards for fifth grade, but will also provide an opportunity for parents to play a larger role in their children's overall education. Finally, the pedagogical stance of these workbooks will allow Barron's publishing to reach a wider audience. It is our view that it is not only parents and their children who will be able to use these books, but also tutors and teachers!

Lisa Wilson, M.Ed
Amy Owens, NBCT El. Ed

Common Core Standards for English Language Arts

The following explanation of educational goals is based on Common Core English Language Arts standards that your child will learn in the fifth grade. A comprehensive list of the Common Core State Standards can be viewed at the following website: *www.corestandards.org*.

Understanding Standard Labels:

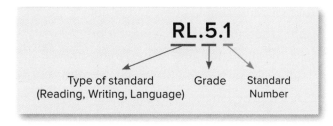

RL.5.1

Type of standard (Reading, Writing, Language) — Grade — Standard Number

Reading Standards

(RF–Reading Foundational Skills / RI–Reading Informational Texts / RL–Reading Literature)

Fluency

(Standards RF.5.4a - RF.5.4.c)

Your student will do/learn the following:

- Read grade-level text with purpose and understanding
- Read on-level prose and poetry with accuracy, appropriate rate, and expression
- Use context to confirm or self-correct word recognition and understanding, rereading as necessary

Key Ideas and Details

(Standards RI.5.1, RI.5.2, RI.5.3, RL.5.1, RL.5.2, and RL.5.3)

Your student will do/learn the following:

- Quote accurately from a text when explaining what a text says explicitly and what can be inferred from the text
- Determine two or more main ideas of an informational text, explain how details support the main idea, and summarize what he or she reads

- Explain relationships between people, events, and ideas in informational texts
- Determine the theme of a literary text from the details in the text
- Compare and contrast two or more characters, settings, or events in a literary text

Craft and Structure

(Standards RI.5.4, RI.5.5, RI.5.6, RL.5.4, RL.5.5, and RL.5.6)

Your student will do/learn the following:

- Define academic and domain-specific words and phrases in informational texts
- Compare and contrast passages from informational texts
- Note similarities and differences in the point of view in informational texts
- Determine meanings of words and phrases, including figurative language, in literary texts
- Explain how chapters, scenes, or stanzas fit together in literary texts to tell a story
- Describe how a narrator's or speaker's point of view influences events in a literary text

Integration of Knowledge and Ideas

(Standards RI.5.7, RI.5.8, RI.5.9, RL.5.7, and RL.5.9)

Your student will do/learn the following:

- Use information from multiple sources to answer questions and solve problems
- Explain how an author uses reasons and evidence to support points in an informational text

- Integrate information from several informational texts in order to write or speak about a subject
- Analyze how visual elements add to the meaning, tone, or beauty of a literary text
- Compare and contrast literary stories in the same genre

Writing Standards (W)

Text Types and Purposes
(Standards W.5.1, W.5.2, and W.5.3)

Your student will do/learn the following:

- Write opinion essays that include: introducing a topic; stating an opinion; supporting an opinion with reasons and evidence; using language to link reasons; and providing a conclusion that restates the opinion
- Write informative/explanatory essays that include: introducing a topic; providing observation and focus; grouping related information; using formatting, illustrations, and multimedia when useful; developing the topics with facts, definitions, concrete details, and examples; using language to link ideas; using precise language and domain-specific vocabulary; and providing a conclusion
- Write narrative essays that include: establishing the story, introducing a narrator and/or character; using precise language and details to describe experiences; using dialogue, pacing, and description to develop events; using transition words to sequence events; using concrete words, phrases, and sensory details to convey experiences and events; and providing a conclusion

Production and Distribution of Writing
(Standards W.5.4, W.5.5, and W.5.6)

Your student will do/learn the following:

- Produce clear and coherent writing (opinion essays, informative essays, and narrative essays) with appropriate organization and purpose
- Develop and strengthen writing by planning, revising, editing, and rewriting
- Use technology, including the Internet, to produce and publish writing

Research to Build and Present Knowledge
(Standards W.5.7, W.5.8, and W.5.9)

Your student will do/learn the following:

- Conduct research to investigate different aspects of a topic
- Gather information from a variety of sources and take research notes and create a list of sources
- Draw evidence from literary and informational texts to analyze, reflect, and research
- Apply reading standards for informational and literary texts to writing (for example, write a compare-and-contrast essay on literature characters, or explain in writing how an author uses reasons and evidence to support a point)

Language Standards (L)

Conventions of Standard English
(Standards L.5.1a–L.5.1e, and L.5.2a–L.5.2e)

Your student will do/learn the following:

- Correctly use conjunctions, prepositions, and interjections in sentences
- Correctly use the perfect verb tenses and use verb tense to convey times, sequences, states, and conditions
- Recognize and correct inappropriate shifts in verb tense
- Correctly use correlative conjunctions (either/or, neither/nor)
- Correctly use punctuation with items in a series

- Correctly use commas with introductory elements and to set off words, tag questions, and direct addresses in sentences
- Use underlining, quotation marks, or italics for titles of works
- Spell grade-appropriate words correctly

Knowledge of Language
(Standards L5.3a and L5.3b)

Your student will do/learn the following:

- Revise sentences by expanding, combining, and reducing them for better meaning and style
- Examine varieties of language used in literary texts, including dialects and other differences

Vocabulary Acquisition and Use
(Standards L.5.4a–L.5.4c and L.5.5a–L.5.5c)

Your student will do/learn the following:

- Use context clues to determine the meaning of a word
- Use Greek and Latin affixes and roots to determine the meaning of a word or phrase
- Use dictionaries and other reference materials to find the pronunciation and determine the meaning of words and phrases
- Examine and show understanding of figurative language, such as similes and metaphors
- Recognize and explain common idioms, adages, and proverbs
- Use relationships between words to better understand those words (synonyms, antonyms, homographs)

Contents

Reading:
Foundational Skills

Fluency: Read with Purpose and Understanding

In this first section, you will work with an adult to help you develop and practice the art of fluent reading. You will practice reading aloud correctly, with ease and good expression.

Reading properly with expression and with as few mistakes as possible is important for your reading progress. Why? Think about this. Fluency provides a connection between recognizing and understanding words. When reading quietly, fluent readers will group words together so that they recognize them right away. When reading aloud, there is a natural quality to their reading that is full of expression.

Whether you are a fluent reader already or are working toward this goal, keep practicing so that you continue to grow in your reading abilities.

Let's begin!

Adults:

While your student is reading, time him or her for one minute and mark any words that were missed by writing the word or crossing it out. When you get to one minute, note where your student has stopped, but allow him or her to continue the story. Fifth graders should be able to read 120–150 words per minute. Count the total number of errors and subtract that from the number of words read. This will give you the total number of words read per minute.

TOTAL NUMBER OF WORDS – NUMBER OF ERRORS = WORDS READ PER MINUTE

Over an extended period of time, your student's fluency, the number of words read per minute, should increase.

Unit 1 (September)	Unit 4 (December)	Unit 7 (March)	Unit 10 (June)
120	130	140	150

Lady Liberty

A woman dressed in a robe and sandals stands in the middle of New York Harbor 16
and has welcomed immigrants from around the world to the United States since 29
1886. She is called the Statue of Liberty or "Lady Liberty." Lady Liberty was a 44
100th birthday gift to the United States from France. 53

Lady Liberty has become a symbol of the United States. Between 1892 and 66
1954, she welcomed more than twelve million immigrants to the nation. 77
To raise money for the construction of the statue's pedestal, Emma 88
Lazarus wrote a poem that illustrates what the statue has come to 100
mean to many immigrants to the United States. The famous poem is 112
now engraved on Lady Liberty's pedestal. Part of that poem reads: 123

Here at our sea-washed, sunset gates shall stand 131
A mighty woman with a torch, whose flame 139
Is the imprisoned lightning, and her name 146
Mother of **Exiles**. From her beacon-hand 152
Glows the world-wide welcome; her mild eyes command 160
The air-bridged harbor that twin cities frame. 167
"Keep, ancient lands, your storied **pomp**!" cries she 175
With silent lips. "Give me your tired, your poor, 184
Your huddled masses yearning to breathe free, 191
The wretched **refuse** of your **teeming** shore. 198
Send these, the homeless, **tempest-tost** to me, 205
I lift my lamp beside the golden door." 213

Words read in 1 minute — errors = WPM

glossary

Exiles: People who have been barred from their native country

Pomp: A show of magnificence

Refuse: Trash or garbage

Teeming: Full of or swarming with

Tempest: A violent, windy storm ("tempest-tost" means tossed in a tempest.)

CHECK FOR UNDERSTANDING

Adults: After your student has finished reading ask him or her to tell you what the passage was about. Your student's response will let you know if he or she understood what was read. Write what your student says about the passage for your own notes.

_____

_____

_____

GUIDED QUESTIONS

Use the information in the passage "Lady Liberty" to answer the questions below.

1. Why was the Statue of Liberty first built?

_____

_____

2. What has the Statue of Liberty come to represent?

_____

_____

3. What purpose does the Statue of Liberty serve in New York Harbor?

_____

_____

4. Give **two examples** from the poem that made you feel the Statue of Liberty was important?

_____

_____

_____

Log Canoes

For more than three centuries, the log canoe was essential to life on the Chesapeake   15
Bay in Virginia and Maryland. These boats were originally built by the native Powhatan   29
(Pow-HAT-un) tribes along the Chesapeake. The canoes were made of logs from pine   42
and poplar trees. Long **troughs** were slowly burned along the length of the logs, and   57
the ashes were scraped from the inside with shells. This made the log into a boat shape   74
with a **hull** and a place for people to sit. The size of the finished canoe depended on   93
the size of the log. Some canoes were thirty feet long and up to three feet wide. They   111
usually carried between ten and thirty people and goods. The Powhatan tribes used   125
these log canoes to navigate and fish along the Chesapeake waterways.   134

    When the English colonists founded Jamestown in 1607, they were amazed by   146
these boats! They decided to add sails to them to increase the speed of the boats. These   163
became the workboats of the Chesapeake Bay because they were inexpensive to build,   176
and the supplies were easy to obtain. Some builders even used several logs to make   191
canoes with multiple hulls. These were able to carry more goods, such as oysters and   206
tobacco. Eventually, these boats were used in racing competitions. Many log-boat   218
racing competitions are still held in the northern part of the Chesapeake Bay. Maybe   232
someday you will have a chance to see one!   241

Words read in 1 minute – errors = WPM

glossary

Hull: The hollow, lowermost portion of a ship

Trough: Any long depression or hollow, as between two ridges or waves

CHECK FOR UNDERSTANDING

Adults: After your student has finished reading ask him or her to tell you what the passage was about. Your student's response will let you know if he or she understood what was read. Write what your student says about the passage for your own notes.

_____

_____

_____

GUIDED QUESTIONS

Use the information in the passage "Log Canoes" to answer the questions below.

1. How did the Powhatans make the log canoes?

_____

_____

2. Why did these boats become the workboats of the Chesapeake Bay?

_____

_____

3. How did the Powhatans and the English colonists use the log canoes?

_____

_____

4. In what **two ways** did the English colonists change the log canoe?

_____

_____

_____

_____

This Is the Pits!

Carlos was so excited to tell his mother about the school field	12
trip that he jumped off the yellow school bus and ran all the way	26
home. His class had gone to the La Brea (bray-uh) Tar Pits in Los	40
Angeles. Carlos had always been fascinated by extinct Ice Age	50
mammals and reptiles.	53

"Slow down, Carlos!" his mother exclaimed when he came 62
through the door breathless. 66

After making a snack, Carlos and his mom sat down at the 78
kitchen table to talk about all of the fascinating things he had 90
learned on the field trip. 95

"Did you know that the only complete skull of a saber-toothed tiger in the entire 110
world was found at the tar pits?" asked Carlos excitedly. "And, they also have the largest 126
collection of **extinct** Ice Age plants and animals in the world!" exclaimed Carlos. 139

"How did all those animals get there?" asked his mom. 149

"Well," Carlos explained, "the tar pits are made from asphalt, a thick, black, gooey 163
substance that can trap even the most powerful animals. The scientist who led our tour 178
said that weak and injured animals would become trapped in the pits, and that would 193
draw larger **predators** to the area. Then they would get trapped, too!" 205

"Oh, that sounds very sad," said Carlos's mother. "But I guess it is good that scientists 221
are able to study all those fossil remains." 229

Then Carlos came up with a great idea. "Hey, mom! Scientists still **excavate** the tar 244
pits, and they have an observatory where visitors can watch them work. Maybe we could 259
go there sometime!" 262

Words read in 1 minute — errors = WPM

glossary

Excavate: To uncover (something) by digging away and removing the earth that covers it

Extinct: No longer existing

Mammals: A type of animal that feeds milk to its young and that usually has hair or fur covering most of its skin

Predators: An animal that lives by killing and eating other animals

Adults: After your student has finished reading ask him or her to tell you what the passage was about. Your student's response will let you know if he or she understood what was read. Write what your student says about the passage for your own notes.

_____

_____

_____

GUIDED QUESTIONS

Use the information in the passage "This Is the Pits!" to answer the questions below.

1. What are the La Brea Tar Pits known for?

_____

_____

2. What is the thick black substance at the pits?

_____

_____

3. How did so many animal remains end up at the pits?

_____

_____

4. What do you think is the most interesting thing that Carlos learned on the field trip?

_____

_____

_____

_____

Lua Pele

The state of Hawaii is a series of islands located in the 12
Pacific Ocean that are actually part of a chain of volcanoes 23
that began to form more than seventy million years ago. 34
The Earth's crust is made up of plates that each moves a 45
few inches every year. The areas where magma (fluid 54
molten rock) pushes these plates apart in the middle of 64
oceans are called **hot spots**. Hot spots often result in 74
volcanoes from which magma erupts in the form of lava. 84
Lava is the red-orange substance that spills out of a volcano 95
onto the Earth's surface. Each Hawaiian Island is made up of one or more volcanoes that 111
originally erupted on the sea floor. After many eruptions, theses volcanoes finally emerged 124
above the ocean's surface. The hot spot is presently located under the Big Island of Hawaii, 140
which is made up of five major volcanoes. This means that the volcanoes on this island 156
still erupt and are considered active. Native Hawaiians call volcanoes Lua Pele 168
(loo-ah peh-leh). One of the volcanoes, or Lua Pele, on the Big Island is Mauna Loa 184
(maw-nuh loh-uh), the largest active volcano on Earth. Another is Kilauea 195
(keel-ah-way-ah), which erupts more lava every year than other volcanoes. Each 206
of these volcanoes erupts every two or three years, but the eruptions are not very explosive. 222
The lava flows are slow enough to allow people plenty of time to reach safety. 237

Words read in 1 minute – errors = WPM

Adults: After your student has finished reading ask him or her to tell you what the passage was about. Your student's response will let you know if he or she understood what was read. Write what your student says about the passage for your own notes.

_____

_____

_____

GUIDED QUESTIONS

Use the information in the passage "Lua Pele" to answer the questions below.

1. Where are the Hawaiian Islands?

_____

_____

2. What made the Hawaiian Islands?

_____

_____

3. What are **hot spots**?

_____

_____

4. What does it mean when a volcano is said to be active?

_____

_____

_____

_____

_____

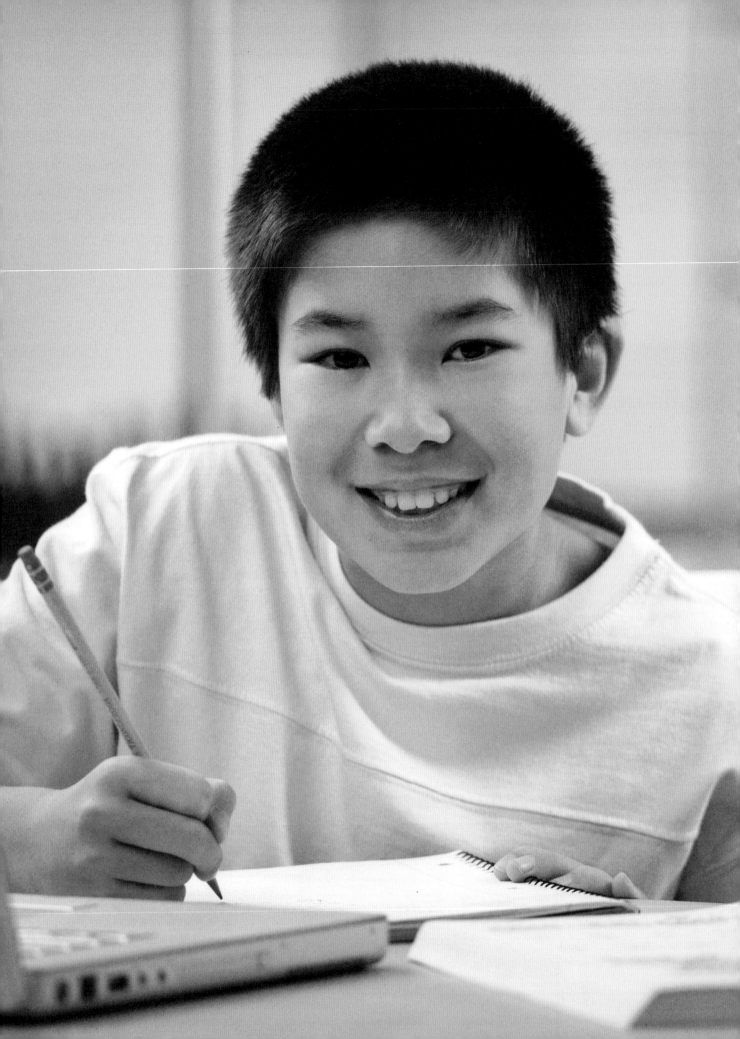

Reading and Writing: Informational Texts

Making History

Being able to read informational passages and understand their meaning is an important quality of a successful reader.

In this section, you will read a variety of historical material. The passages and activities will test your ability to understand the information by having you answer questions based on what is directly stated as well as what may be only suggested in the texts. Read the passage first so that you can pick out the main ideas. Look for other features such as the author's tone and point of view, as well as the organization of the passage. Refer back to the appropriate areas in the text as you work out the answers to each question.

Using the details presented, sharpen your reasoning abilities to write about what you learn. Writing will help you to clarify new information by building upon what you know and what you feel to be true, or your opinion.

Let's begin!

Father of Our Country

Early Life

Have you ever heard the tale of the boy who was able to throw a silver dollar all the way across the Potomac River? Or have you heard the tale about the young boy who tried out his new ax by cutting down his father's prized cherry tree? This boy later admitted his naughty deeds and became famous for saying, "I cannot tell a lie." These are both tales about a boy named George Washington. Not much is known about his early years, yet many tales such as these have been told about his young life. However, what is known for sure is that Washington was born in Virginia on February 22, 1732, and that he grew into a man with outstanding leadership ability and came to be greatly respected by many.

Military Life to Mount Vernon

As a young man, Washington served in the Virginia **militia** in the French and Indian War. A few years later, he earned an honorable title by being appointed commander of all the Virginia troops at the tender age of twenty-three. It was obvious that Washington was a natural-born leader. After the war, Washington returned to his home, Mount Vernon, in 1758 and married Martha Dandridge Custis. Eventually, Washington became involved in government matters and was elected to the Virginia colony government.

Birth of a Nation

As the strain increased between the colonies and the English government, Washington helped create the Continental Congress that first met in 1774. Members from twelve of the thirteen colonies attended. This meeting was the very beginning of our own government. The battles of Lexington and Concord in April 1775 marked the start of the American Revolution. At a meeting of the second Continental Congress in Philadelphia, Pennsylvania, Washington was made Commander-in-Chief of the colonial soldiers. Two very important things happened next. First, in May of 1776, Washington and two others from a secret group of the Continental Congress visited a Philadelphia **seamstress** named Betsy Ross. They asked her to sew a flag to represent the colonies. The flag she designed was adopted as the first official colonial flag. Then, on July 4, 1776, the Continental Congress signed the Declaration of Independence. By signing this document, they announced that the colonies were no longer under the control of the British government. Washington was finally able to lead the colonists to victory against the British, who surrendered after the Battle of Yorktown in 1781. It had taken six long years, but a nation was finally born!

First President

The new nation was struggling. The colonies were fighting among themselves. None of them could agree on state boundaries or who would pay for the cost of the war they had just won. Luckily, a new formal plan for our government, known as the Constitution, was written in 1787 at a special meeting in Philadelphia. It united the colonies under a central government. They soon stopped fighting with each other. Two years later, members of the Continental Congress selected Washington to be the very first President of the United States. He became a great leader who solved many of the young nation's problems. He went on to serve two terms as president and is now fondly known as the "Father of Our Country."

glossary

Militia: A group of citizens organized for military service

Seamstress: A woman who sews clothes, curtains, and other things as a job

FINDING MAIN IDEAS AND DETAILS

After reading "Father of Our Country," answer the questions below.

1. What is this passage mainly about? Identify **two main ideas** found in the text.

_____

_____

_____

_____

2. Select a key detail that supports one of the main ideas from this text.

    A. Washington served two terms as president of the United States.

    B. The Constitution was written at a special meeting in Philadelphia, Pennsylvania.

    C. Washington married Martha Dandridge Custis in 1758 when he returned home to Mount Vernon.

    D. The first meeting of the Continental Congress was the beginning of our government.

3. Which key detail supports another main idea of this passage?

   A. Washington served in the Virginia militia in the French and Indian War.

   B. Washington helped create the Continental Congress that first met in 1774.

   C. At the battle of Yorktown in 1781, Washington led the victory against the British.

   D. Washington and two others from the Continental Congress asked Betsy Ross to sew the first American flag.

4. Write a sentence or two to explain how the following things and people are related:

           Betsy Ross's flag   First Continental Congress

           George Washington   Constitution

   _____

   _____

   _____

   _____

5. When did the United States declare itself an independent country? Use quotes from the passage to support your answer. Remember to use quotation marks around any text taken from the passage.

   _____

   _____

   _____

   _____

   _____

   _____

   _____

   _____

USING CONJUNCTIONS

Conjunctions are joiners, or words that connect parts of a sentence together.

for   and   nor   but   or   yet   so

It might be helpful to remember the conjunctions this way:

FANBOYS: For - **A**nd - **N**or - **B**ut - **O**r - **Y**et - **S**o

Conjunctions join words, phrases, and clauses.

Words: Individual or paired words.

Phrases: A group of two or more words that does not have a subject (noun or pronoun) and verb combination.

Clauses: Groups of words that have a subject (noun or pronoun) and a verb combination.

Examples:

Washington was an outstanding military leader and government official.

Washington led the new nation to victory against the British but the colonies were still struggling.

The colonies were fighting, but a new plan for government united them.

Underline the conjunctions in each of the following sentences. Tell whether the conjunction is joining words (W), phrases (P), or clauses (C). Write your answer on the line provided.

1. Washington and a secret group from the Continental Congress visited a Philadelphia seamstress named Betsy Ross. _____

2. Not much is known about Washington's early years, yet many tales have been told about his young life. _____

3. The strain increased between the colonies and the English government. _____
_____

4. It had taken six long years, but a nation was finally born! _____

5. He served two terms as the president and is now known as the "Father of Our Country."

_____

Challenge: Can you combine these two sentences using a conjunction? Write your answer on the lines provided. Remember that a comma goes before the conjunction when combining sentences.

Washington and a secret group from the Continental Congress visited a Philadelphia seamstress named Betsy Ross. They asked her to sew the very first American flag.

_____

_____

_____

Correlative conjunctions are pairs of conjunctions that are always used together. They connect balanced words, phrases, and clauses.

either ---> or   neither ---> nor   not only ---> but ---> also

Example: Neither George nor Martha Washington realized they would one day be famous.

Which pair of correlative conjunctions best completes each sentence? Use what you have learned from the text to make each sentence make sense. Write your answers on the lines provided.

1. Washington was _____ a military hero _____

    first President of the United States.

2. From all historic reports, Washington was _____ a proud

    _____ a boastful man.

3. _____ were colonists tired of paying British taxes _____

    were tired of living under British rules.

4. George Washington could _____ retire to his home in Mount Vernon

    _____ accept the position as president.

Cross out any extra words or phrases in the following sentences. If necessary, write in a word to replace them.

1. The battle of Yorktown was fought in Yorktown, which is a town in Virginia.

2. The secret group from the Continental Congress asked Betsy Ross, who was a Philadelphia seamstress, to sew the first flag.

3. George Washington is considered the father of our country due to the fact that he was involved in many events that led to our independence.

4. As a result of the fact that the British surrendered at Yorktown, the colonists won independence.

5. The tales of Washington's activities in his youth are interesting, but it is unlikely that those stories are all true.

Challenge: Can you revise these sentences by combining them? Write your revision on the lines provided.

The Colonial soldiers did not have uniforms and wore their own clothes. They also brought along their own food and equipment. The British soldiers did have regular uniforms.

_____

_____

_____

_____

_____

_____

_____

Replace the bolded word in each sentence by circling the adjective or adverb that would make each sentence more interesting and clear. Consult a dictionary if you need to determine the definition of a word.

1. The battle at Yorktown was **difficult**.

   (fierce or hard)

2. Washington often longed for the **quiet** life at Mount Vernon.

   (boring or peaceful)

3. There are many **invented** tales about George Washington.

   (fanciful or created)

4. The Continental Congress **eagerly** voted for Washington to be the first president.

   (enthusiastically or quietly)

5. George Washington and his army **strongly** faced all challenges.

   (bravely or valiantly)

Digging Deeper

If you want to learn more about the uniforms and equipment worn and used by Colonial and British soldiers during the Revolutionary War, visit the following website: *www.nps. gov/mima/forteachers/upload /essentials.pdf*

Standard L.5.3.a, L.5.4.c

Unfurling a Legend

Is the charming story about Betsy Ross sewing the first American flag just that—a charming story? Or does the fact that it has been a part of American education for over a century prove that is has true meaning?

Early Life

Betsy Ross was born Elizabeth Griscom on January 1, 1752, in Philadelphia to Samuel and Rebecca Griscom. After attending school, Ross became an **apprentice** for an **upholsterer** named William Webster. In Webster's workshop, she learned to make a variety of things like mattresses, chair covers, rugs, and window blinds. It was here that Ross met another apprentice, John Ross, who later became her husband. The two were married in 1773 and started their own upholstery shop. Ross became very well known for her work throughout the colonies.

The Flag

Surprisingly, Ross did not become famous for making the first American flag until many years later. In 1877, her grandson, William J. Canby, described her story to the Historical Society of Pennsylvania. He shared that Ross often told the family about an important visit she received in May 1776 from a secret committee of the **Continental Congress**. This committee was made up of three men: George Washington, George Ross, and Robert Morris. These men asked her to make the first official flag of the colonies. Washington showed Ross a rough design for the flag that included six-pointed stars. He asked if she could make a flag to look like it. In response, Ross showed the secret committee how to cut a perfect five-pointed star with one snip of the scissors! Admiring her talent, they hired her for the job. Not long after this visit, Ross completed the sewing of the first flag. The flag had thirteen alternating red and white stripes and thirteen white stars on a blue background. Each of those stars and each of those stripes represented one of the thirteen colonies. This flag was adopted by the Continental Congress as the first official flag of the colonies in June of 1777.

The Debate

Some historians question whether the story told by Ross's grandson is true because there are no written records about the first flag. The newspapers of the day did not even mention this meaningful event. Yet, others believe the first flag was, indeed, made by Ross for a number of reasons. For example, Ross told many other family members the same story she had told her grandson. Each family member gave the same exact details about Ross's story of the night she was visited by the secret committee. Also, Ross personally knew the three members of the secret committee who visited her because they all attended the same church. She had even done other sewing work for them. This may have been one of the reasons she was chosen to sew the flag. Finally, many upholsterers took work making tents, uniforms, and flags during wartime to make money.

One record shows that Ross was paid a large sum of money from the Pennsylvania State Navy Board for making flags. In any event, it is well documented that Ross was a talented upholsterer, and she continued to make flags for the rest of her life.

Today, schools across the nation tell the Betsy Ross story and historical societies continue to publish it. However, we may never really know for sure if Betsy Ross did, in fact, sew the very first American flag. What do you think?

EXPAND YOUR KNOWLEDGE:

There were many women besides Betsy Ross who played important roles in the American Revolution. To start learning more about them and the amazing things they did, you can visit the following website:

www.americanrevolution.org/women/women.html

FINDING MAIN IDEAS AND DETAILS

After reading "Unfurling a Legend," answer the questions below.

1. List **two main ideas** found in this passage.

    _____

    _____

    _____

    _____

2. List two different key details to support each main idea that you have identified in question 1.

    _____

    _____

    _____

    _____

RELATIONSHIPS BETWEEN INDIVIDUALS IN THE TEXT

Write a sentence using the following words, explaining how they are related.

Betsy Ross, First Continental Congress, George Washington

_____

_____

_____

_____

_____

_____

COMPARING AND CONTRASTING TEXTS

After reading both "Father of Our Country" on page 23 and "Unfurling a Legend" on page 31, compare the way the two texts are written. Then, answer the questions below.

1. Is the text "Father of Our Country" fiction or nonfiction? How can you tell?

   _____

   _____

2. Is the text,"Unfurling a Legend" fiction or nonfiction? How can you tell?

   _____

   _____

3. How are "Unfurling a Legend" and "Father of Our Country" mainly structured?

   _____

   _____

4. Read the following sentences from "Father of Our Country."

   "As a young man, Washington served in the Virginia militia in the French and Indian War. A few years later, he earned an honorable title by being appointed commander of all the Virginia troops at the tender age of twenty-three."

   Read the following sentences from "Unfurling a Legend."

   "In response, Ross showed the secret committee how to cut a perfect five-pointed star with one snip of the scissors! Admiring her talent, they hired her for the job."

   Do the sentences from "Father of Our Country" and "Unfurling a Legend," have the same or different text structures? Explain.

   _____

   _____

   _____

   _____

   _____

Standard RI.5.5

UNDERSTANDING INTRODUCTORY ELEMENTS

Introductory elements are phrases and words that appear before the main part of the sentence.

- They prepare readers for what the sentence is really about.
- They can be taken away from the sentence, and the sentence still makes sense.
- They are followed by a comma.

Examples: Made in 1776, the colonial flag has thirteen stars.
To tour the Betsy Ross house, you need to visit Philadelphia.

Underline the introductory element and place a comma after it in each of the following sentences.

1. In order to earn money during the war many upholsterers took work sewing tents and flags.

2. Well known in Philadelphia for her beautiful sewing work Betsy Ross was asked to make the very first American flag.

3. Showing the men how to make a perfect five-point star with one snip of the scissors Betsy Ross was able to convince them to hire her.

4. After the war she continued to make flags.

5. Representing each of the colonies thirteen individual white stars are featured on a field of blue.

UNDERSTANDING ITEMS IN A SERIES

- A series is a list of three or more items or things of the same type (**words**, **phrases**, or **clauses**).

- A conjunction (**and**, **or**, **nor**) goes between the last two items of the series.

- The items are separated by commas.

> Example: The flag is red, white, and blue.
>
> It might be helpful to remember the following formula:
>
> # of items – 1 = # of commas

In each of the following sentences, circle the items, underline the conjunction, and add the commas where they belong.

1. The three men on the secret committee were George Washington Robert Morris and George Ross.

2. The flag had a field of blue thirteen white stars and thirteen alternating red and white stripes.

3. Many upholsterers took work making tents uniforms or flags during wartime to make money.

4. Neither Betsy her children nor her grandchildren realized she would become an American legend for simply sewing a flag.

5. Betsy Ross learned how to sew mattresses chair covers and window blinds.

WRITE YOUR EXPLANATION

After reading "Unfurling a Legend" on page 31, use the organizer to plan a short essay explaining the life of Betsy Ross and why she is an important historical figure.

Title: _____

Introduction (Topic sentence stating the main idea)

_____

_____

_____

_____

_____

_____

_____

_____

Supporting Detail (Use a detail from the text)

_____

_____

_____

_____

_____

_____

_____

_____

Standard W.5.2.a–e

Supporting Detail (Use a detail from the text)

_____

_____

_____

_____

_____

_____

Supporting Detail (Use a detail from the text)

_____

_____

_____

_____

_____

_____

Conclusion (A few sentences restating the main idea)

_____

_____

_____

_____

_____

_____

Taking Flight

In this next unit, you will read about extraordinary people who dedicated their lives to advancing the field of aviation. They are forever remembered for their bravery, their heroic flights, and the legacies they left behind.

In the Clouds

1   Imagine flying like a bird high above the clouds into the vast blue sky with the rush of the wind whistling past your ears! As a young boy, that is exactly what Charles Lindbergh dreamed of doing. When he got older, he entered flight school in 1922 to make his dream come true. One of his first jobs was as a **wing walker**, performing extremely daring stunts. He also worked as an airplane mechanic. Lindbergh bought his very own plane in 1923 and began flying as a solo pilot. He went on to become an airmail pilot for the U.S. Postal Service in 1926. He regularly flew between the cities of Chicago and St. Louis. It was during this time as an airmail pilot that Lindbergh earned the nickname "Lucky Lindy" because he had to parachute from his plane to safety more than once! He was living his dream of flying, but his biggest achievement was yet to come.

2   Airplanes were a fairly new invention in the 1920s, and many people were interested in flying. A St. Louis businessman offered a prize of $25,000 to the first pilot who could fly nonstop between New York City and Paris, France. Lindbergh wanted to be the pilot to win that prize. As a result, he convinced a group of businessmen to pay for his flight.

3   Lindbergh even helped to design a single-engine plane for the trip and named it the *Spirit of St. Louis*. On his way to New York City from San Diego, California, he set a flight record. Lindbergh reached his destination in fourteen hours and twenty-five minutes.

4   Newspapers nicknamed Lindbergh the "Flying Fool." No one thought Lindbergh would be able to make the flight to Paris because he was flying alone in a single-engine plane. The flight would be long, and there was the danger that he could fall asleep. However, the biggest challenge Lindbergh faced was getting his plane off the ground because it carried so much heavy fuel. He knew he was up against a difficult task. Lindbergh took off in the *Spirit of St. Louis* from New York on May 20, 1927. He finally arrived at the airfield in Paris thirty-three and a half hours later. That's more hours than there are in one whole day!

Around the world, Lindbergh became known as the first pilot to fly nonstop between New York and Paris.

5   Four million people showed up for a parade in his honor when he returned to America. Lindbergh was awarded the Congressional Medal of Honor and the very first Distinguished Flying Cross award.

6   After his famous flight, Lindbergh did many other things to advance the field of **aviation**. He advised airline companies on how to make new air travel routes in unknown places. During World War II, he worked as a test pilot and helped with studies on altitude and body temperature. He even flew in combat missions! A few years later, Lindbergh won the Pulitzer Prize, a yearly prize awarded to authors, for his 1953 book about his famous flight.

7   Today, Lindbergh's famous plane, the *Spirit of St. Louis*, is on display for all to see at the National Air and Space Museum in Washington, D.C. The young boy who once dreamed of flying in the clouds became a groundbreaking pilot who will always be best remembered as the first solo pilot to cross the Atlantic Ocean in 1927.

FINDING MAIN IDEAS AND DETAILS

After reading "In the Clouds," answer the questions below.

1. What is the **main idea** of the article?

   A. Charles Lindbergh helped design and build the Spirit of St. Louis.

   B. Charles Lindbergh attended several flight schools to learn to fly.

   C. Charles Lindbergh was a pioneer pilot who advanced aviation.

   D. Charles Lindbergh helped the U.S. government during World War II.

2. Which key detail **best** supports the main idea of the article?

   A. Charles Lindbergh had to parachute to safety while working as an airmail pilot.

   B. Charles Lindbergh won the Pulitzer Prize for his book about his famous flight.

   C. Charles Lindbergh became an airmail pilot in 1926 and flew between two cities.

   D. Charles Lindbergh was the first solo pilot to fly nonstop between New York and Paris.

3. What is the **main idea** of the third paragraph?

   A. The flight from New York to Paris was very long.

   B. Single-engine planes carried many gallons of fuel.

   C. Lindbergh faced many challenges in making the flight from New York to Paris.

   D. Lindbergh was nicknamed the "Flying Fool" because it was not possible to make the flight.

4. Which **key detail** supports the main idea of the third paragraph?

   A. Lindbergh designed the *Spirit of St. Louis* for his trip to Paris.

   B. Lindbergh convinced a group of businessmen to pay for his trip.

   C. Lindbergh earned the nickname "Lucky Lindy."

   D. Lindbergh earned the nickname the "Flying Fool."

 Standard RI.5.1, RI. 5.2

5. What quote from the text **best** explains why Charles Lindbergh became a world-famous hero? Use evidence from the text to support your answer.

_____

_____

_____

_____

_____

_____

_____

_____

_____

6. Explain why others did not think that Charles Lindbergh could successfully make the flight from New York to Paris. Use evidence from the text to support your answer.

_____

_____

_____

_____

_____

_____

_____

_____

_____

UNDERSTANDING VOCABULARY

After reading "In the Clouds," answer the questions below.

1. Define **aviation**. Use a dictionary to find the meaning and write your answer below.

_____

_____

_____

2. What are **wing walkers**? Use clues from the story to help you understand what this word means. Write your answer below.

_____

_____

_____

RECOGNIZING SYNONYMS

A synonym is a word that suggests the same meaning as another word.

Circle the synonym of the bolded word in each sentence.

1. He was living his dream of flying, but his biggest **achievement** was yet to come.

(triumph or defeat)

2. He **advised** airline companies on how to make new air travel routes in unknown places.

(considered or informed)

3. He bought his first plane in 1923 and began flying as a **solo** pilot.

(accompanied or unassisted)

4. Lindbergh did many things to **advance** the field of flying.

(further or limit)

5. Lindbergh was a **groundbreaking** pilot who will be best remembered as the first solo pilot to cross the Atlantic Ocean.

(famous or revolutionary)

WRITE YOUR ESSAY

Imagine that you are a wing walker at an air show! Write an essay about your experience. Remember to add details from the five senses to make your essay more interesting. What do you feel? What sensations make you feel good? Does anything make you uneasy? Use the graphic organizer to help you map out your essay.

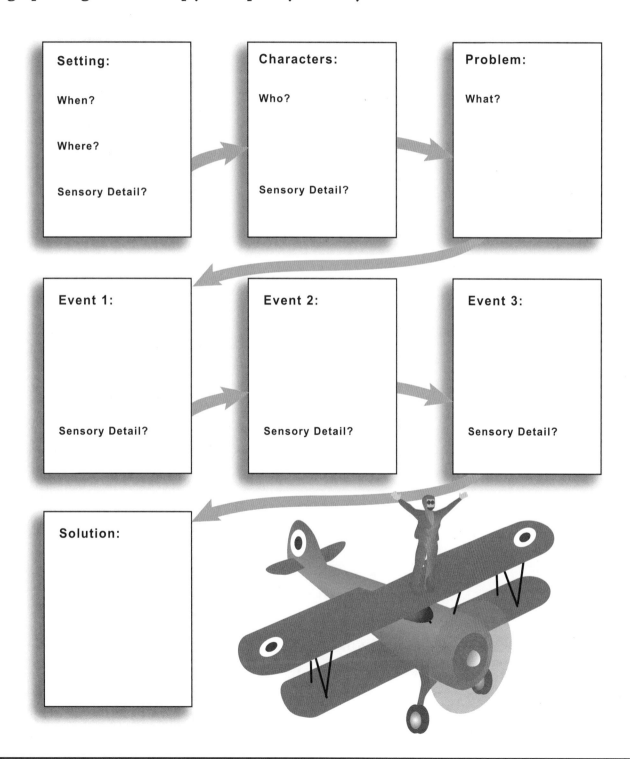

Setting:

When?

Where?

Sensory Detail?

Characters:

Who?

Sensory Detail?

Problem:

What?

Event 1:

Sensory Detail?

Event 2:

Sensory Detail?

Event 3:

Sensory Detail?

Solution:

Soaring to the Skies

1 "As soon as I left the ground, I knew I myself had to fly." Those were the words of Amelia Earhart after she took her very first ride in an airplane in 1920. She had instantly fallen in love with flying! Earhart took flying lessons and earned her flying license by the end of 1921. She bought her very first airplane and named it *Canary*. Earhart set her first flight record by flying all the way up to 14,000 feet. That is a little more than two and a half miles off the ground! As a result, Earhart became the sixteenth woman in history to earn an international pilot's license in 1923. These achievements were extra special because there were very few female pilots at that time.

2 Earhart was part of a special trip in 1928. She was invited as the very first female passenger ever to take a **transatlantic** flight. Today, planes are able to cross the Atlantic Ocean in about seven hours. In 1928, it took over twenty hours to make that same journey! After a successful trip, Earhart arrived back in New York City and was compared to the famous American pilot, Charles Lindbergh. She was given the nickname "Lady Lindy." All over the country Amelia Earhart was recognized as a famous celebrity!

3 Earhart used her fame to create the organization called The Ninety-Nines in 1929. The name is just as it sounds. The Ninety-Nines was a group of ninety-nine female pilots formed for the purpose of supporting women who had an interest in flying. A couple of years later, Earhart went on to become the very first female pilot to fly across the Atlantic Ocean in 1932. Vice-President Charles Curtis presented her with a **Distinguished Flying Cross Award** for making that flight. Just a few years after this in 1935, Earhart became the first person to fly solo across the Pacific Ocean from Hawaii to California. After all of these wonderful achievements, Earhart set even higher goals for herself.

4 Earhart planned to become the first female pilot to fly around the world. She and her co-pilot took off from Miami, Florida, to begin this world flight in June of 1937. Their first stop was on the island of New Guinea. As they continued on, they left from New Guinea on July 1st headed for Howland Island in the middle of the Pacific Ocean. However, their plane never arrived on the island. The United States Navy searched for them for two weeks without success.

5   Earhart soared to the skies as a **pioneer** of flight who encouraged women to work in the field of aviation. The Ninety-Nines organization that she helped create still exists today and has thousands of members around the world. The members are female professional pilots, flight instructors, and mechanics. All over the world, Earhart will always be remembered as a role model for women in the field of aviation.

FINDING MAIN IDEAS AND DETAILS

After reading "Soaring to the Skies," answer the questions below.

1. What would be another good title for this article?
   A. "Amelia Earhart the Flight Pioneer"
   B. "The Disappearance of Amelia Earhart"
   C. "Amelia Earhart's Many Flying Adventures"
   D. "Crossing the Ocean with Amelia Earhart"

glossary

Pioneer: A person who is the first to do or explore something

2. Circle the sentence that contains the **best** supporting detail for the title you identified in question 1.
   A. Amelia Earhart took flying lessons in 1921.
   B. Amelia Earhart rode her first plane in 1920.
   C. Amelia Earhart was the very first female pilot to fly across the Atlantic Ocean.
   D. Amelia Earhart was a leader in the field of aviation in the twentieth century.

3. What is another **main idea** from this article?
   A. Amelia Earhart set many flight records.
   B. Amelia Earhart won an international pilot's license.
   C. Amelia Earhart was invited on a transatlantic flight.
   D. Amelia Earhart encouraged women to work in the field of aviation.

4. Which statement provides a supporting detail for the main idea identified in question 3?
   A. Amelia Earhart was given the nickname "Lady Lindy."
   B. Amelia Earhart formed The Ninety-Nines organization.
   C. Amelia Earhart was the first person to fly alone across the Pacific Ocean.
   D. Amelia Earhart planned to become the first woman pilot to fly around the world.

5. What quote from the text **best** explains why Amelia Earhart first became nationally famous? Cite your example from the text below, remembering to use quotation marks for material taken directly from the text.

_____

_____

_____

_____

_____

_____

_____

_____

_____

_____

6. Explain what event made Amelia Earhart want to make a flight across the Atlantic Ocean alone.

_____

_____

_____

_____

_____

_____

_____

_____

1. What is the **Distinguished Flying Cross award**? Use reference materials such as an encyclopedia or the Internet to find out and write your answer below.

_____

_____

_____

2. What does the term **transatlantic** mean? Use clues from the story to help you understand what this word means. Write your answer below.

_____

_____

RECOGNIZING ANTONYMS

An antonym is one word that has the opposite meaning of another word.

Circle the antonym of the bold word in each sentence.

1. These achievements were **special** because there were few female pilots at that time.
   (typical or exceptional)

2. She helped **create** an organization called The Ninety-Nines.
   (form or demolish)

3. Fuel and repair stops were **scheduled** along the way.
   (undetermined or anticipated)

4. Amelia Earhart is most **remembered** for this flight.
   (overlooked or recalled)

5. Amelia Earhart also used her fame to help other women become more **involved** in flying.
   (engaged or disconnected)

WRITE YOUR OPINION

Explain why you think the contributions of Charles Lindbergh and Amelia Earhart are an important part of history. What did they do that has a lasting impact on our lives today? Use the graphic organizer to help you state your opinion and organize your reasons. Cite evidence from the text to support your belief.

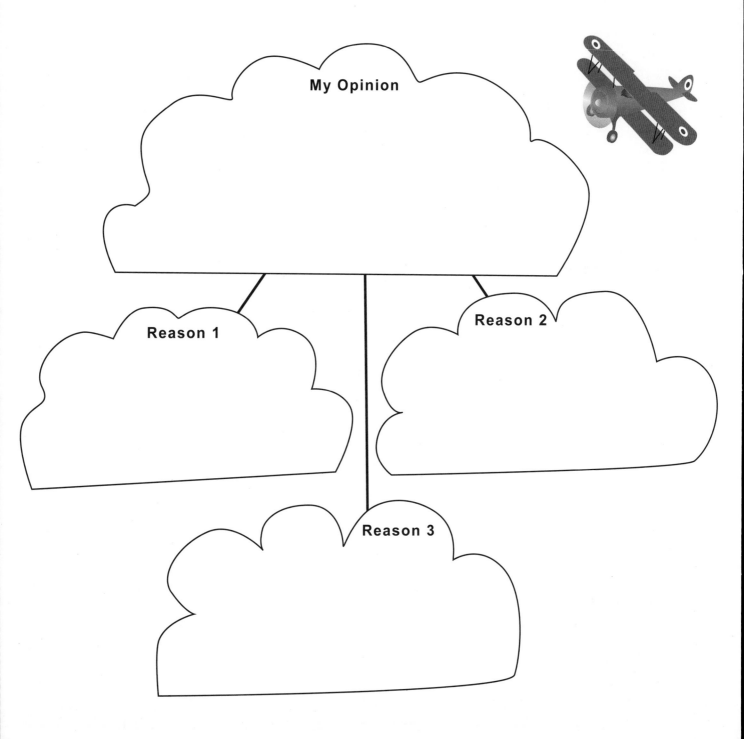

My Opinion

Reason 1

Reason 2

Reason 3

Standard W.5.1.a–d

Use the following outline to write a draft of your opinion essay on the importance of Charles Lindbergh and Amelia Earhart. Remember to use transition words and phrases to connect your ideas!

> **Transition words and phrases:**
>
> | | | | | |
> |---|---|---|---|---|
> | also | because | first | second | third |
> | another | in addition | for example | such as | therefore |

Introduction: State your opinion and list your reasons.

_____

_____

Paragraph 1: State your first reason and explain it with facts and details.

_____

_____

Paragraph 2: State your second reason and explain it with facts and details.

_____

_____

Paragraph 3: State your third reason and explain it with facts and details.

_____

_____

Concluding Paragraph: Write a conclusion and be sure to restate your opinion and reasons.

_____

_____

_____

Helping People

I am sure you have helped someone in your life—perhaps you have helped your parents with housework, or maybe you have helped a friend study for a test, or you may have helped a baby do something that he or she could not do alone. In each of these situations when you helped someone, how did you feel?

Imagine helping a group of people or an entire country to obtain legal rights to do important things. In this next unit, you will read about two heroic women who will always be remembered for the positive changes they created for America.

A Fearless Leader

1   Have you ever seen a one-dollar coin like this one? It's a Susan B. Anthony coin that was first made in 1979 to honor Susan Brownell Anthony for her lifelong devotion to the struggle for women's equality. Born in 1820 in Adams, Massachusetts, Anthony would become famous for the role she played in fighting for women's right to vote.

2   She also should be remembered for the important roles she played in the **antislavery** movement and in improvements to education.

3   After Susan B. Anthony's family moved to Rochester, New York, in 1845, the entire family became very active in the abolitionist movement. They hosted antislavery meetings at their farm every Sunday. They were often joined by Frederick Douglass, an escaped slave who went on to become a famous author and political figure. Anthony became a member of the Anti-Slavery Society in 1856 and dealt with angry mobs and threats as she arranged antislavery meetings and made speeches calling for the end of slavery. In 1863, she helped organize the Women's National Loyal League to petition for the outlawing of slavery with the Thirteenth Amendment. This amendment was finally passed, and Anthony continued to fight for full citizenship and voting rights for both African-Americans and women.

4   The first paying job that Susan B. Anthony held was in education. She taught in a few schools in New York before finally arriving at Canajoharie Academy in 1846. She worked as a female principal at the academy for two years and became involved in the teacher's union when she discovered that male teachers were paid $10.00 per month while female teachers were only paid $2.50 per month. She later spoke at a state teachers' convention and called for better pay for female teachers and for women to be allowed to choose any type of employment. Additionally, Anthony fought for educational opportunities for all people. She urged public schools and colleges to admit women and ex-slaves. One positive result of Anthony's work was that the University of Rochester finally admitted women for the first time in 1900.

5   Most of all, Susan B. Anthony is known as a leader of the women's **suffrage** movement. Before 1920, women were not allowed to vote. The suffragist movement began to change that law. The female members of this movement were called suffragettes. Susan B. Anthony traveled around the country giving speeches and setting up women's rights organizations. In 1872, Anthony voted in the November election and wrote that she voted "the straight Republican ticket." She was later arrested for voting illegally in a federal election and was ordered by the judge at her trial to pay a $100 fine. In 1878, she successfully introduced a constitutional **amendment** on the women's right to vote to Congress. The bill did not pass, but she continued to appear before congress every year until around 1902 to convince them to pass this amendment. Sadly, Anthony died in 1906 and never saw her goal fulfilled. Finally, in 1920, the Nineteenth Amendment to the United States Constitution, also known as the Susan B. Anthony amendment, was passed and allowed women the right to vote.

6   The next time you hold a Susan B. Anthony coin, think about all the hard work she did on behalf of the rights of all people. Remember that she not only did a lot for the women's movement, but she also helped with the abolitionist movement and to improve education!

glossary

Amendment: to change the meaning of a bill or law

FINDING MAIN IDEAS AND DETAILS

After reading "A Fearless Leader," answer the questions below.

1. What are **two main ideas** of the passage? Write your answer on the lines below.

_____

_____

_____

2. Circle the sentence that contains the **best** supporting detail of one of the main ideas from the passage.

   A. Anthony's family moved to Rochester, New York, in 1845.

   B. Anthony taught in New York and was a female principal at Canajoharie Academy.

   C. Anthony appeared in Congress to convince them to pass a suffrage amendment.

   D. Women were not allowed to vote in elections before 1920.

Use evidence from the text to answer the following questions.

3. According to the author of "A Fearless Leader," what are the three important reasons you should remember Susan B. Anthony? List the reasons below.

   Reason 1: _____

   Reason 2: _____

   Reason 3: _____

4. List one piece of evidence that the author uses to support each one of the reasons.

   Evidence to support reason 1: _____

   _____

   Evidence to support reason 2:_____

   _____

   Evidence to support reason 3:_____

   _____

USING CONJUNCTIONS

- Subordinating conjunctions are used to join two clauses—usually an independent clause (complete thought) and a dependent clause.

- A clause that a subordinating conjunction introduces is called "subordinate" or dependent because it cannot stand by itself as a sentence.

- The subordinating clause usually answers questions (when or why?) about the main clause or imposes conditions on the main clause.

Example: I can go outside to play after I finish my homework.

Independent clause   subordinating conjunction and subordinate clause

Note: Sometimes the independent clause comes first in the sentence, and sometimes the subordinating conjunction and subordinate clause come first. Place a comma after the subordinate clause if it appears first.

Some common subordinating conjunctions are listed here:

| before | since | after | because | even though | since |
| if | whenever | unless | once | rather than | until |

Underline the subordinating conjunction and the subordinate (dependent) clause in each of the sentences.

1. After the Anthony family moved to Rochester, they became involved in the antislavery movement.

2. Susan B. Anthony was a teacher before becoming a female principal.

3. Even though Anthony spent the majority of her life fighting for women's right to vote, she did not live to see the Nineteenth Amendment passed into law.

4. Women now enjoy the right to vote because of the efforts by people like Susan B. Anthony.

5. Until 1920, women were not permitted to vote in elections

Challenge: Subordinating conjunctions are used to join two ideas. Use a subordinating conjunction to join these two clauses together. Write your answer on the line.

Susan B. Anthony went to jail. Susan B. Anthony voted in the 1872 election.

Using context clues or a dictionary, answer the questions below.

1. What does the term **suffrage** mean? Use clues from the passage to help you understand what this word means. Write your answer below.

   _____

   _____

2. What was the **antislavery** movement? Use reference materials such as an encyclopedia or the Internet to find out and write your answer below.

   _____

   _____

REVISING SENTENCES

Cross out any extra words or phrases in the following sentences. If necessary, write in a word to replace them. Combine and rearrange sentences when you can.

1. Susan B. Anthony was arrested and jailed. Susan B. Anthony voted in the 1872 election.

   _____

2. Susan B. Anthony dealt with angry mobs when she arranged antislavery meetings. Susan B. Anthony was very active in the abolitionist movement.

   _____

3. Susan B. Anthony worked in the field of education as a teacher and as a female principal at Canajoharie Academy, which is in New York.

   _____

4. The Susan B. Anthony coin was first made in 1979. Susan B. Anthony's likeness appears on a coin to honor her work in the struggle for women's equality.

   _____

The Conductor

1   Born into slavery on the eastern shore of Maryland, Harriet Tubman eventually gained fame as a "conductor" on the Underground Railroad. What most people don't know is that in addition to helping escaped slaves reach freedom in the North, Harriet Tubman worked as a spy for the Union during the Civil War, and as a nurse as well. People should remember and respect her efforts in these other areas too.

2   In 1849 at the age of twenty-nine, Harriet Tubman gained her freedom by running away to Philadelphia, which is north of the **Mason-Dixon Line**. Once there, she worked as a housemaid until she earned enough money and had enough contacts to go back and rescue several of her family members. This marked her very first trip back onto southern soil to lead other slaves to freedom on what was called the Underground Railroad. The Underground Railroad was a series of secret routes and safe houses that led escaped slaves to freedom. Tubman spent the next ten years as a "conductor" on this railroad and made a total of nineteen trips, freeing about three hundred people.

3   To make these historic trips, Harriet Tubman used many clever ideas. She would escape with the slaves on a Saturday night because runaway-slave notices could not be placed in newspapers until Monday morning. She used disguises and once had male fugitives dress as women because it had been announced that a group of male slaves had escaped from a plantation. Another time, she bought a ticket on a train going south to outsmart those who were pursuing her. She figured they would only look for her on northbound trains, and she was right! Tubman was one of the Underground Railroad's best conductors, and her capture would have brought a $40,000 reward from the South. Harriet Tubman also took part in many antislavery meetings and became friends with

other leading abolitionists such as Frederick Douglass. Douglass once said, "I know of no one who has willingly encountered more **perils** and hardships to serve our enslaved people than [Harriet Tubman]."

4   In addition to her work on the Underground Railroad, Harriet Tubman also acted as a spy and was the first woman in American history to lead a military **expedition**. She had a lot of knowledge of the different towns and transportation routes of the South. This knowledge was very useful to the Union troops. Also, Tubman often dressed as an old woman and wandered the streets of towns under Confederate control as a spy for the Union. There, she met many slaves who provided her with information about Confederate troop placement and supply lines. In 1863, Tubman and Colonel James Montgomery led 150 black soldiers on a gunboat raid in South Carolina. Information given to her by her scouts allowed them to surprise the Confederates and free about 750 slaves!

5   Finally, Harriet Tubman worked as a nurse during the war to heal the sick and injured. She used many folk and herbal remedies in her treatments, which provided relief to patients. After the war, she dedicated her time to helping former slaves, especially children and the elderly. She created the Home for the Aged in Auburn, New York, for the care of elderly African-Americans. Tubman was also very active in the women's movement and was considered a suffragist. When her own health declined, she was cared for at the Home for the Aged, where she died in 1913 from pneumonia.

6   Considered the first African-American woman to serve in the military, Tubman was buried with military honors. This famous "conductor" of the Underground Railroad should not only be remembered for her work in freeing slaves, but also for all the work she did for the Union Army and for those who were unable to care for themselves.

glossary

Expedition: A trip organized for a particular purpose

Peril: A danger of injury, pain, or harm

FINDING MAIN IDEAS AND DETAILS

After reading "The Conductor," answer the questions below.

1. What are **two main ideas** of the passage? Write your answer on the lines below.

_____

_____

_____

2. Circle the sentence that contains the **best** supporting detail of one of the main ideas from the passage.

  A. Tubman was born a slave in Maryland.

  B. Tubman helped with a gunboat raid in South Carolina.

  C. Tubman escaped to Pennsylvania at the age of 29.

  D. Tubman died in New York in 1913.

USING REASONS AND EVIDENCE

1. According to the author of "The Conductor," what are the three important reasons you should remember Harriet Tubman? List the reasons below.

  Reason 1: _____

  Reason 2: _____

  Reason 3: _____

2. Below, list one piece of evidence that the author uses to support each one of the reasons.

  Evidence to support reason 1: _____

  _____

  Evidence to support reason 2: _____

  _____

  Evidence to support reason 3: _____

  _____

COMPARING STRUCTURE

Compare the texts "A Fearless Leader" and "The Conductor." Answer the questions and complete the activity below.

1. What is the structure of both passages? Circle the letter of the best answer.
    A. problem/solution
    B. cause/effect
    C. comparison
    D. chronology

2. Which key words from both passages helped you to determine the structure of both passages?

    _____

    _____

3. Complete a flow chart for each passage. List the **most** important events from each passage in the order in which they occurred.

"A Fearless Leader"

"The Conductor"

USING REFERENCE MATERIALS

What is the **Mason-Dixon Line** and how is it related to the Civil War? Use reference materials such as an encyclopedia or the Internet to find out and write your answer below.

_____

_____

_____

RELATIONSHIPS BETWEEN WORDS—SYNONYMS

Circle the synonym of the bolded word in each sentence.

1. Harriet Tubman used many **clever** techniques to help escaped slaves reach freedom.

   (witty or foolish)

2. Tubman became friends with other **leading** abolitionists.

   (unknown or noted)

3. Tubman worked as a nurse and used folk and herbal **remedies**.

   (medicine or disease)

4. Her work in other areas should be **respected**.

   (admired or ignored)

5. Southern slaves **provided** Tubman with useful information.

   (refused or gave)

6. After the war, Harriet Tubman cared for the **elderly**.

   (old or young)

Digging Deeper

The Underground Railroad was an organized system to assist escaped slaves reach freedom in the North. It was a network of people, secret routes, and safe houses. Visit this website to watch a short video to learn more about Underground Railroad: *http://video.pbs.org/video/1479874539*

Use your imagination to create a new character who fights for the rights of others. Who will your character be, and what traits will he or she have? For what right will your character struggle, and what problems will he or she encounter? Your character could choose to work for the right of all students to have computers or for the right of all animals to have loving homes. Write a story about your character and his or her experience. Use the graphic organizer to help you map out your story.

Setting:

Conflict (Problem):

PLOT

Event 1:

Event 2:

Event 3:

Climax (Major event that changes the course of the story):

Resolution (Conclusion):

REVIEW

Congratulations! You have completed the lessons in this section. Now you will have the chance to practice some of the skills you just learned.

Reading Fluency

Adults: Time your student for one minute while he or she is reading to you. Make a note of where he or she is after one minute to track your student's fluency. (Your student should be able to read 120–150 words per minute.) Have your student continue reading to the end of the passage in order to answer the questions that follow.

Presidents' Day

Every year on the third Monday of February, we celebrate something called	12
Presidents' Day. It's a little confusing, though, because the holiday started	23
out as a celebration of George Washington's birthday. In fact, in 1879 it	36
became **official** with a vote in Congress, and George Washington became the	48
first person to be honored with a federal holiday. Historians say that George	61
Washington's birthday was February 11, 1732, but a change in the calendar	73
system twenty years later shifted all dates by eleven days. So, Washington's	85
birthday became February 22. It was celebrated on this date for many years.	98

In 1968, President Johnson signed what is called the Uniform Monday Holiday Act, which	112
shifted several holidays, including Veteran's Day, Memorial Day, and Washington's Birthday to	124
Mondays. It was hoped that the change would create more three-day weekends so that American	139
workers could spend more time with their families. The Uniform Monday Holiday Act also	153
included the idea that the holiday should be a combined celebration of George Washington's	167
birthday and Abraham Lincoln's birthday. This made sense because Lincoln was also born	180
in February. Even though Lincoln was included, the official name of the holiday was still "George	196
Washington's Birthday."	198

Many people believed that the holiday should be officially renamed and called "Presidents'	211
Day," to honor Lincoln for his role in saving our nation during the Civil War and helping to free	230
the slaves. Some states even went as far as to rename the holiday "Presidents' Day." Other	246
people feel that calling it "Presidents' Day" takes the focus away from our founding father,	261
George Washington, and that future generations will not grasp how important he was to our	276

nation. There have even been federal laws introduced to Congress to require the nationwide use   291
of the term "George Washington's Birthday." None of these laws has passed. What do you   306
think? Should the holiday be celebrated for just George Washington, or should all presidents   320
be honored on this holiday for their service to our nation?   331

Words read in 1 minute – errors = WPM

Activity 1

Underline the conjunction in each of the following sentences. Tell whether the conjunction is joining words (W), phrases (P), or clauses (C). Write your answer on the line provided.

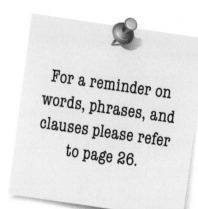

For a reminder on words, phrases, and clauses please refer to page 26.

1. Citizens agree that we should celebrate the holiday, but what should it be called? _____

2. People feel Abraham Lincoln should be honored for his role in preserving the nation and helping to free slaves. _____

3. George Washington and Abraham Lincoln were both born in the month of February. _____

4. Presidential historians say George Washington was born on February 11, so we don't really celebrate Presidents' Day on his real birthday. _____

Activity 2

Circle the antonym of the bolded word in each sentence. Use a dictionary if you need a better understanding of a word meaning.

1. Americans began publicly **celebrating** Washington's birthday.

    (overlooking or honoring)

2. Historians say the **actual** date of George Washington's birth is February 11, 1732.

    (uncertain or definite)

3. Some people feel Lincoln should be honored for his role in **preserving** the nation.

    (protecting or harming)

4. Many people believe that calling the holiday "Presidents' Day" is **shifting** the focus away from the father of our country.

    (changing or keeping)

UNDERSTAND

After reading "Presidents' Day," answer the questions below.

1. In the space below, write the **main idea** of "Presidents' Day."

_____

_____

_____

_____

_____

2. In the space below, write **two key details** that support the main idea.

_____

_____

_____

_____

_____

3. What quote from "Presidents' Day" best explains why some people believe that only Washington's birthday should be honored? Cite your example from the text below, remembering to use quotation marks around material taken from the text.

_____

_____

_____

_____

_____

4. The Uniform Monday Holiday Act served to encourage what two important purposes in the lives of Americans?

_____

_____

_____

5. Read the following sentence from the article. What does the bolded word mean?

    *"In fact, in 1879 it became **official** with a vote in Congress, and George Washington became the first person to be honored with a federal holiday."*

_____

_____

_____

_____

6. Use the word **official** in a sentence of your own.

_____

_____

_____

_____

DISCOVER

What would you say? Let's take what you learned and write about it!

Write Your Opinion

Imagine that the United States Congress is trying to decide which president should be honored on Presidents' Day. Some people are saying that only Washington should be honored, others say that Washington and Lincoln should be honored, while still others say that all past presidents should be honored.

Take a position on this issue and write a letter to your state's senator. Explain your opinion and support it with at least two strong reasons.

Gathering Information:

Step 1:   Reread the article "Presidents' Day."

Step 2:   Find out who your state's senators are by visiting the following website:
www.senate.gov/general/contact_information/senators_cfm.cfm
Be sure to write down the senator's name and address!

Step 3:   Ask an adult to help you search on the Internet for at least one article about the topic of Presidents' Day. *Hint:* A good search engine to use is *www.google.com,* and you might use the phrase "Presidents' Day controversy" in your search.

Step 4:   Read the article you located and take some notes on it. You can use some of the ideas and reasons you found to help you form your own opinion and reasons.

Starting to Write:

Step 5:   Use the graphic organizer to state your opinion and organize your reasons.

Step 6:   Take the information from your graphic organizer and write out your opinion and reasons in complete sentences. Be sure to include transition words and phrases to link your ideas!

Step 7:   Ask an adult to read what you have written. Work together to do the following:

- Make sure you have presented your opinion and two reasons clearly.
- Look for places where you can make better word choices.
- Proofread your paper for errors in grammar and mechanics.
- Pay special attention to commas with introductory elements and items in a series.

Step 8:   Now you are ready to write your letter! Here is what you need to do:

- Begin by dating the letter, addressing the senator, and telling a little bit about yourself.
- Next, write your opinion and reasons.
- Ask an adult to help you address the envelope so that you can mail it.
- Sign your letter.

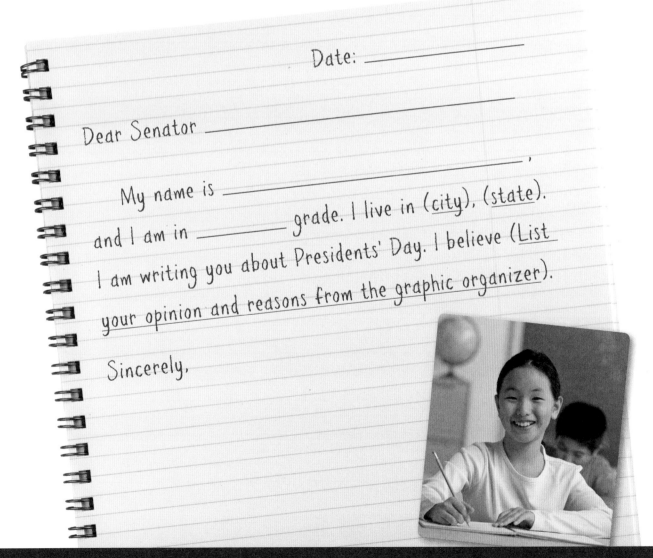

Date: _____

Dear Senator _____,

My name is _____ and I am in _____ grade. I live in (city), (state). I am writing you about Presidents' Day. I believe (List your opinion and reasons from the graphic organizer).

Sincerely,

Write Your Opinion

> **Transition words you might choose to use::**
>
> first   second   next   also   finally
>
> *Remember to use commas after transition words that begin sentences!

Use the organizer to state your opinion and reasons.

My opinion is: _____

_____

_____.

Reason #1. I think (your opinion) because (list reason #1)

_____

_____.

Supporting detail: _____

_____.

Supporting detail: _____

_____.

Reason #2. It is my belief (your opinion) because (list reason #2)

_____

_____.

Supporting detail: _____

_____.

Supporting detail: _____

_____.

Our Land

Earth is a beautiful jewel in the midst of our vast universe. In this next unit, you will read about important places in America that hold the key to the survival and balance of Earth's ecosystem.

Extreme Conditions

1   Imagine a place where there are sand dunes as high as 600 feet tall and where the temperature might get as hot as 120°F! Well, there is such a place right here in the United States called the Mojave (moh-hah-vee) Desert. The Mojave Desert is the smallest of the four North American deserts and was named after the Mojave tribe of Native Americans. It stretches across parts of four states—California, Nevada, Utah, and Arizona. Sadly, the territory of the Mojave Desert faces several dangers due to urban

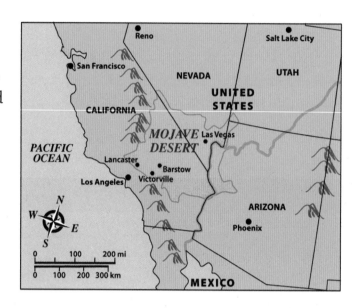

and agricultural growth, the need for more **landfill** space, and off-road-vehicle recreation. The Mojave Desert should be saved because it is home to unique land structures, plants, and animals that are found nowhere else in the world, and it produces a lot of economic activity and tourism.

2   The Mojave Desert is fascinating because it has many elevation extremes and special land features. The range of elevations in the Mojave is not found in any other desert in North America. Death Valley, located in the Mojave Desert, is 282 feet below sea level and is not only the lowest point in the Western Hemisphere but also the hottest place in North America. Some of the mountains in the Mojave are over 5,000 feet tall. Another really striking feature of the Mojave Desert is the Kelso Dunes, which are sand dunes that can reach up to 600 feet in height. Amazingly, these dunes make a unique, almost barking sound when people run down the sides of them. It is thought that the countless grains of sand rubbing against each other causes this sound.

3   The Mojave Desert is home to close to 2,500 species of plants and animals, and more than 100 of these species are thought to be **endangered** wildlife. Also, about one-fourth of these plants and animals are native to the Mojave Desert, which means that they are found nowhere else in the world. The Joshua tree, which is a spike-leafed evergreen, only

grows in the Mojave Desert. Scientists think that some of the Joshua trees are up to 500 years old. Some of the animals native to the Mojave Desert include the Mojave ground squirrel, the amargosa vole, which is a mouse-like rodent, the California leaf-nosed bat, and the relict leopard frog. Although it doesn't just live in the Mojave, the desert tortoise lives in the region and is listed as an endangered species.

4   Even though it is a desert, the Mojave is home to over one million people, and another forty million live within a day's drive of it. Tourism is an important business in the area. There are several national parks in the area that generate this tourism. The most popular spots include the Mojave National Preserve, the Joshua Tree National Park, and Death Valley. Additionally, there are several ghost towns in the region, such as Calico and Bodie, which are left over from the gold and silver rush eras. These ghost towns serve as fun sightseeing attractions. Some mining, including the mining of silver, tungsten, and iron, still takes place in the region and is an important form of local business. Also, borax, potash, and salt are extracted from an area called the Central Salt Flats. These industries help the economy of the Mojave region.

5   While the habitat of the Mojave Desert is badly affected by human activity, around half of this desert remains in its original, beautiful condition. However, the landfills planned for the cities of Los Angeles and San Diego, and ongoing damage from off-road vehicles, are current problems for the area. The efforts to save the Mojave Desert should be continued because this region is home to special land features, plants, and animals that are found nowhere else in the world, and the area brings in a lot of economic activity and tourism.

glossary

Endangered: When an animal is in danger of dying off completely

Landfill: A site where garbage is put

EXPLAINING RELATIONSHIPS

After reading "Extreme Conditions," answer the following questions.

1. Using evidence from the text, explain the relationship between the national parks and the Mojave Desert region.

_____

_____

_____

2. Using evidence from the text, explain why protecting the Mojave is important to species such as the Joshua tree or the Mojave ground squirrel.

_____

_____

_____

QUOTING FROM THE TEXT

3. Explain how the Mojave Desert is important to people. Cite a specific example from the text.

_____

_____

_____

EXPLAINING REASONS AND EVIDENCE

After reading "Extreme Conditions," complete the reading idea web.

Here are some questions to help you get started:

1. What was the passage about? What was the author's opinion?
2. Why is the topic important? What reasons did the author provide?

Main

____

____

____

Reason

____

____

____

Reason

____

____

____

Reason

____

____

____

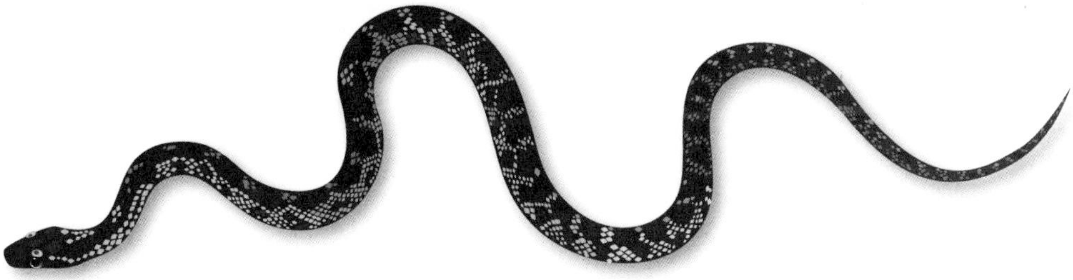

UNDERSTANDING HOMOGRAPHS

Homographs are words that are written or spelled exactly the same way, but have different meanings and sometimes different pronunciations. *Hint:* Use context clues to decide the meaning and pronunciation of homographs.

Example: The word **bow** is a homograph.

He tied a bow on the present. He took a bow after the performance.

1. Since lots of **wind** blows in the Mojave Desert, wind farms have been set up to generate power.
   A. to loop or turn   B. movement of air

2. There were so many mosquitoes that I had to **bat** them away.
   A. to hit at   B. flying mammal

3. My friend visited the Mojave National **Preserve** when she was in California.
   A. to keep safe   B. an area where plants and animals are protected

4. Let's hope the farmers along the Colorado River in the Mojave region never **desert** their crops.
   A. to leave   B. a warm, dry area with little vegetation

5. The Colorado River **winds** through an eastern part of the Mojave Desert.
   A. to loop or turn   B. movement of air

6. Native Americans used the **bark** of the Joshua tree for bowls and dishes.
   A. the sound a dog makes   B. a tough covering of root or stem

7. We should **preserve** the Mojave Desert because it is a unique habitat.
   A. to keep safe   B. an area where plants and animals are protected

8. The California leaf-nosed **bat** only lives in the Mojave Desert.
   A. to hit at   B. flying mammal

9. Death Valley, the hottest place in North America, is in the Mojave **Desert**.
   A. to leave   B. a warm, dry area with little vegetation

10. The Kelso Dunes will **bark** if people run down the sides of them.
    A. to make the sound of a dog   B. tough covering of root or stem

"It's all Greek to me" is a phrase people use when they don't understand something. Many of the words we speak in the English language, however, have their origins in ancient languages. Learning to recognize Greek or Latin root words and affixes (prefixes and suffixes) makes it easier to tell the word's meaning.

> **Example:** What is the meaning of geology? Look at the Greek root word and the Greek suffix for your answer:
>
> **Root word:** geo- = earth
>
> **Suffix:** -ology (or logy) = science or study of something
>
> geo + [o]logy = geology= the science or study of the Earth

Prefix	Root word	Suffix	Meaning	Origin	Example	Meaning of example
	aud		to hear	Latin	auditorium	a place where people go to hear a performance or speech
semi-			half	Latin	semisweet	partly sweet
		-ence	act or state of	Latin	excellence	the act of being excellent (high quality)
auto-			self	Greek	autograph	signature written by one's hand
	photo		light	Greek	photocopy	a copy of an image made by the action of light on an electrically charged surface
		-ologist	one who studies	Greek	zoologist	one who studies zoology (the study of animals and animal life)

Read the paragraph and circle the words that have Greek or Latin affixes or root words. Then, write the word next to its definition.

Many geologists exhibit a great deal of intelligence in their work. Some of them go to the Mojave Desert with their automatic cameras. They set it to take photographs of rocks and sand dunes. Sometimes they have an audience of prairie dogs standing in a semicircle.

_____ A. A group who gathers to hear something

_____ B. Self-acting, or acting on its own

_____ C. One who studies the history of Earth, especially rocks

_____ D. A picture made by means of a camera that directs the image of an object on film that is sensitive to light

_____ E. A half of a circle

National Treasure

1   When you think of national treasures, you may think of things like silver and gold, but there are some treasures that are even more valuable than that! In the United States, we have one such treasure right in the state of Florida. It is called the Everglades.

2   The Everglades is a very special large, freshwater wetland that stretches from Central Florida all the way to the Florida Bay in the south. During the wet season, Lake Okeechobee (oh-ki-choh-bee), which is the largest lake in Florida and the southeastern United States, overflows. This extra water goes into a very slow-moving and shallow river. The water continues to flow to the south and passes through many different types of habitats, including cypress swamps, wet prairie, and mangrove swamps. Eventually it reaches Everglades National Park and the Florida Bay.

3   So, what's the big deal about a bunch of soggy land? Well, wetlands like the Everglades are very important to both animals and people. Wetlands provide important support for wildlife, decrease flooding, and remove pollutants from water. They also provide a place for **recreation**.

4   The Everglades is a complex system of habitats that depend on each other as neighbors. The habitats within the Everglades are created by small changes in land elevation, which is how high the land is above sea level. Some of the most recognizable of these habitats are the sawgrass marshes, the cypress swamps, the mangrove swamps, the pinelands, and the coastal marshes. The Florida Bay is considered to be part of the Everglades because its **habitat** is affected by the Everglades. The freshwater from the Everglades mixes with the salt water of the ocean and creates a unique environment for specific plants and animals to live.

5   Each of the Everglades' habitats forms many different communities of plants and animals. The Everglades has over 1,000 species of plants and is home to 350 species of birds.

6   The Everglades is especially well-known for the many wading birds that live there, such as ibises and spoonbills, because they can survive in the shallow waters. It is also the only natural habitat where alligators and crocodiles can be found living side by side!

7   The Everglades is home to many threatened and endangered species. Some of the threatened and endangered animals and birds that make their homes in the Everglades include the American alligator, the wood stork, the Southern bald eagle, the manatee, and sea turtles. Manatees and sea turtles live in the Florida Bay and feed on the special grasses that grow where the water of the Everglades meets the water of the ocean. The most endangered of the Everglades' animals is the Florida panther. Sadly, there are only about 100 Florida panthers left in the world.

8   The Everglades is also important because it provides the people of South Florida with drinking water and water for farm crops. Wetlands help improve water quality because they filter pollutants out of the water. Believe it or not, the wetlands also help to reduce flooding in other areas. Wetlands act like huge sponges that can trap overflowing water and then slowly release it. This helps prevent flooding during times of heavy rain. The Everglades also gives people a wonderful place to fish, boat, and bird-watch.

9   The Everglades contained over 2.3 million acres of wetlands in the early 1900s. By the 1970s, only about 1.1 million acres remained. In 1934, Congress passed a bill to create the Everglades National Park. It was the first time that a national park had been created for the purpose of preserving animals and plants. Since then, many laws have been passed to not only save but also restore the Everglades. Also, many groups are involved in conservation efforts to save what remains of the Everglades for future generations. The Everglades is being recognized as the national treasure it is!

glossary

Habitat: The natural environment in which plants and animals live

Recreation: Something people do for enjoyment

After reading "National Treasure," answer the next set of questions.

1. Use examples from the text to explain how the wetlands affect the water in southern Florida.

_____

_____

_____

2. Using what you read in the text, explain the relationship between the Everglades and the manatee.

_____

_____

_____

MAKING INFERENCES

3. What would **most** likely happen to the Florida panther if the Everglades disappeared? How do you know? Use evidence from the text to support your answer.

_____

_____

_____

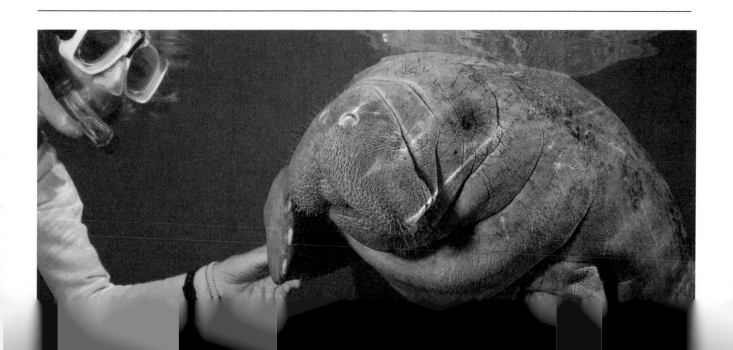

After reading "National Treasure," fill out the reading-cluster diagram. Show how the author uses reasons and evidence to support any opinions expressed in the text.

Here are some questions to help you get started:

1. What was the passage about? What was the author's opinion?

2. Why is the topic important? What reasons did the author provide?

Reason 1

_____

_____

_____

Reason 2

_____

_____

_____

↖ **Main Idea** ↗

_____

_____

_____

↙ ↘

Reason 3

_____

_____

_____

Reason 4

_____

_____

_____

Digging Deeper

To learn more about what people are doing to save the Florida panther, and what you can do to help, read all about it in *Trails & Tails*. Visit:
www.evergladesplan.org/docs/082010_trails_tails_brochure_short.pdf

USING PREFIXES

A *prefix* is a group of letters that is added to the front of a root word to accurately define the meaning of a word.

One example is the word *unhappy.* The prefix *un-* means *not* or *the opposite of.*

un- + *happy* = *not happy*

Prefix	Meaning
re-	again
inter-	between
co-	with, together

Add the correct prefix to the front of each root word to make a new word. *Hint:* You might be able to make more than one new word!

1. store _____

2. dependent _____

3. act _____

4. creation _____

5. exist _____

6. play _____

Use each of the words you just made to complete the following sentences.

1. The wetlands help _____ flooding in other areas.

2. Alligators and crocodiles _____ in the Everglades.

3. The wetlands provide a place for _____ such as boating and fishing.

4. The _____ habitats of the Everglades work together as neighbors.

5. Many laws have been passed to save and _____ the Everglades.

6. The birds and animals of the Everglades _____ with each other and their environment.

After reading "National Treasure," use the organizer to plan a short essay explaining the importance of the Everglades to the animals who live there.

Introduction (the topic sentence that states the main idea):

_____

_____

_____

Supporting Detail (a detail from the text that supports the topic sentence):

_____

_____

_____

Supporting Detail (a detail from the text that supports the topic sentence):

_____

_____

_____

Supporting Detail (a detail from the text that supports the topic sentence):

_____

_____

_____

Conclusion (a concluding sentence that summarizes the main idea):

_____

_____

_____

Our Oceans

The oceans are home to creatures of all shapes and sizes. In this unit, you will read about the importance of oceans and how they affect other forms of life. Additionally, you will learn of one animal that is in need of our help so that it continues to thrive in Earth's oceans.

Streaming

1   Did you know that there is a river right in the middle of the Atlantic Ocean? Well, there is, and it is called the Gulf Stream. The Gulf Stream is a very powerful, warm-water current that is about 50 miles wide, up to 1,500 feet deep, and travels at an average of 4 miles per hour. It starts in the Gulf of Mexico, flows right past the tip of Florida, and picks up speed as it streams past the eastern coast of the United States, where it turns eastward off the coast of North Carolina. From North Carolina, it travels northeast where it joins another current, the North Atlantic Drift, and moves on to places as far as Great Britain and northern Europe!

2   The Gulf Stream is just one of many ocean currents, which are made by wind energy. The wind energy on Earth is concentrated in bands called trade winds that blow from the east to the west, and westerlies, which blow from the west to the east. As the wind blows across the surface of the ocean, it transfers energy to the water, causing the surface water to travel in certain directions. The Gulf Stream is formed by trade winds from Africa that push water in the Atlantic Ocean westward until it

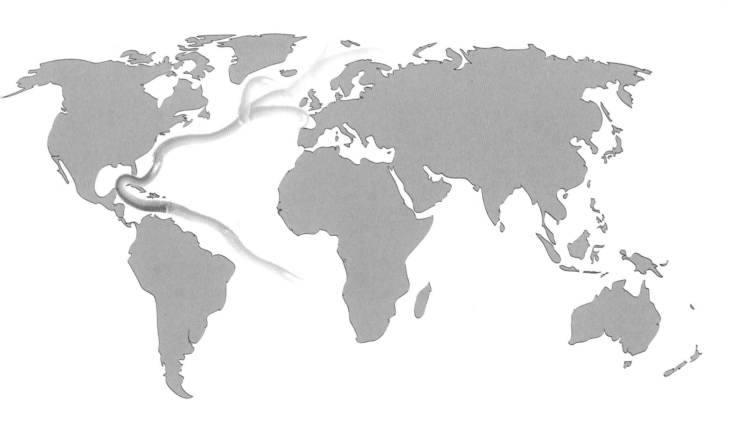

hits the coastline of North America. The water is then pushed northward because it has nowhere else to go. This action produces a river of water right in the middle of the ocean. The Gulf Stream transports about four billion cubic feet of water per second, more than is carried by all the world's rivers combined!

3   Two reasons why the Gulf Stream is important have to do with climate and what lives in the sea. Water has the ability to absorb heat and carry it over great distances before releasing it. The Gulf Stream carries warm water from near the equator to regions much farther north. The heat from the water in the Gulf Stream affects the climates of the areas close to it, such as Florida, and also the far-away regions where it flows, such as Great Britain and northern Europe. That is why places such as Great Britain and northern Europe have milder weather than more southerly locations in North America, such as Chicago.

4   Another important purpose of the Gulf Stream involves its effect on marine life. As the Gulf Stream flows, sections of moving water swirl away from the main current and make whirlpools. These whirlpools are called eddies and contain water that is warmer than the surrounding water. Eddies are usually good fishing areas. There are some places where the Gulf Stream runs into underwater rocky ledges and cliffs and things called seamounts, which are active or extinct underwater volcanoes. These seamounts and underwater cliffs block the flow of the Gulf Stream, which creates turbulence, or roughness, in the water. The turbulence increases plankton growth. Plankton consists of tiny plants that float in the water. Plankton growth attracts small fish that feed on it. The schools of smaller fish draw in larger fish, which then hunt the smaller fish. These areas are great for fishing as a result.

5   This river in the middle of the ocean called the Gulf Stream has a great impact, or effect, on human life. It changes our weather, and it creates areas for good fishing.

After reading "Streaming," answer the questions below.

1. Give an example from the text that helps you determine the relationship between The Gulf Stream and climate.

_____

_____

_____

2. What is the relationship between the Gulf Stream and marine life?

_____

_____

_____

Explain how the Gulf Stream is important to people. Cite a specific example from the text.

_____

_____

_____

_____

Digging Deeper

Trade winds that blow westward from Africa are largely responsible for the Gulf Stream current. If you would like to learn more about the actions in the atmosphere that create the trade winds and the Gulf Stream, visit the following website to watch a video *www.pbslearningmedia.org/resource/ess05.sci.ess.watcyc.gulf-stream/what-causes-the-gulf-stream*

TAG QUESTIONS

Tag questions are phrases added at the end of a sentence that turn the sentence into a question.

- Use a comma to separate the tag question from the rest of the sentence.
- Use a question mark for ending punctuation.

> Example: It's hot out today, isn't it?

Revise the following sentences by including tag questions. Be sure to add any needed punctuation.

1. The Gulf Stream affects the climate.

2. The Gulf Stream isn't in the Pacific Ocean.

3. Small fish will be attracted to the plankton.

4. Eddies contain warmer water than what surrounds them.

5. Seamounts are things that block the flow of the Gulf Stream.

COMMAS WITH DIRECT ADDRESSES

A direct address is when the person who is speaking uses the name of the person to whom he or she is speaking in a sentence. Use commas to separate direct addresses from the rest of the sentence.

> Use one comma if the direct address appears at the beginning or end of the sentence.
> Use two commas if the direct address is in the middle of the sentence.

> Example: Excuse me, sir, can you tell me the time?
> Terry, you were elected class president!

Underline the direct address in each of the following sentences. Add the needed commas.

1. Captain Smith will the fishing be good along the Gulf Stream?

2. The Gulf Stream has an impact on climate Don.

3. The trade winds Maria are what create the Gulf Stream.

4. Did you know John that the Gulf Stream is around fifty miles wide?

5. Aunt Sandra I learned that the water in the Gulf Stream affects marine life.

Standard L.5.2.c

VERB TENSE

Verb tense consistency means using the same, or consistent, verb tense within a sentence. All the verbs in a sentence should refer to the same time period, unless actions in the sentence happened at different times. Shifting verb tense in a sentence often confuses readers.

> **Example:**
>
> **Incorrect:** Carrie **finished** her homework and **watches** TV.
>   (past tense)   (present tense)
>
> **Correct:** Carrie **finished** her homework and **watched** TV.
>   (past tense)   (past tense)

Activity 1

Look for verb tense consistency in the following sentences. Change the second verb to match the tense of the first, underlined verb. Write your answer on the line. If the verbs in the sentence already have the same tense, write "correct" on the line.

1. Trade winds **blow** from east to west, and westerlies blew from west to east.

2. The plankton **attracted** small fish which feed on it.

3. The Gulf Stream **is** about fifty miles wide and travels at an average of four miles per hour.

4. Great Britain and northern Europe **have** mild climates because the Gulf Stream brought warm water to the region.

5. The turbulence in the water **caused** plankton growth, and now many fish eat in the area.

Activity 2

Read these sentences, which all *begin* in the present tense. Circle the verbs that shift to the past tense.

Trade winds blow from Africa and push water in the Atlantic Ocean westward until it hits the coastline of North America. Then the North American coastline pushed the water north, which created a river of water right in the middle of the ocean. We call this river in the ocean the Gulf Stream. The Gulf Stream brings warm water to Great Britain and northern Europe and made the temperatures there milder.

Saving the Sea Turtles

1 Sea turtles are reptiles that have lived in the ocean for millions of years and even managed to survive the changes on Earth that killed the dinosaurs. Sea turtles can be found in all of the world's oceans except in the polar regions. There are seven species of sea turtles, and six of those types are endangered. Some of the main issues that pose a danger to sea turtles are loss of living areas, non-natural lighting, fishing, unlawful trade, and pollution.

2   Turtle eggs and hatchlings face many natural threats. Predators, such as raccoons and crabs, raid turtle egg nests for food. Once baby turtles hatch, they try to make their way to the ocean, but they are often eaten by birds and crabs. Once they are grown,

turtles have few natural predators. The problems they face as adults have a lot to do with human activity.

3   Sea turtles lay their eggs on beaches. Coastal development, or growth, traffic, and human use of beaches for entertainment have destroyed many sea turtle nesting beaches. The artificial lighting from coastal development and tourist areas discourages female turtles from nesting. It can also confuse sea turtle hatchlings. These newly born sea turtles are guided to the sea by the natural light of the moon. When they see artificial lights, they can become mixed up and wander off in the wrong direction. If they travel too far inland, they can die.

4   Each year hundreds of thousands of sea turtles are harmed by the fishing industry. They are caught by mistake in shrimping and fishing nets and on hooks. They become what is called *bycatch*, or unintentionally caught marine life. Because turtles need to breathe on the surface, they drown once they are caught in these nets. Also, sea turtles are purposely caught so their parts, such as the oil and shell, can be used to make products. Often these products are unlawfully traded.

5   Turtles also face the danger of plastic trash pollution, such as plastic bags, bottles, and food wrappers. About eighty percent of this plastic washes out to sea from beaches and streets through storm drains and rivers. Sea turtles often eat these plastic items because they mistake them for food. For instance, sea turtles will eat plastic bags because they look like jellyfish, a main part of their diets. Eating plastic kills sea turtles. These reptiles get caught and tangled in plastic items like fishing line and plastic netting. The result is the same as when turtles are caught in fishing nets.

6   There are many organizations that work hard on solutions to save sea turtles. These organizations work with governments to make stronger laws that protect sea turtles and to form protected areas where sea turtles can safely nest. They also tag turtles so they can use satellites to track their movements. This information tells scientists more about turtle feeding and nesting areas so they can make better choices about how to protect the turtles. Efforts are ongoing to change rules about artificial lighting in certain areas. These organizations also work with the fishing industry to help them switch to using more turtle-friendly equipment to reduce bycatch. Finally, these organizations rely on teaching people to recycle and get rid of garbage properly, to avoid buying banned turtle products, and to turn off lights on beaches. With luck, these efforts will increase worldwide sea turtle populations.

After reading "Saving the Sea Turtles," answer the following questions.

1. What overall idea is the author stating? How do you know?

   _____

   _____

2. Which idea from the passage "Saving the Sea Turtles" does the following piece of evidence support?

   "Sea turtles often eat these plastic items because they mistake them for food."

   A. Sea turtles are illegally hunted.

   B. Sea turtles face many natural threats.

   C. Sea turtles face threats from pollution.

   D. Sea turtles are harmed by the fishing industry.

3. Which idea from the passage "Saving the Sea Turtles" does the following piece of evidence support?

   "They become what is called bycatch, or unintentionally caught marine life."

   A. Sea turtles are illegally hunted.

   B. Sea turtles face many natural threats.

   C. Sea turtles face threats from pollution.

   D. Sea turtles are harmed by the fishing industry.

4. Explain how the following piece of evidence supports one of the ideas the author of "Saving the Sea Turtles" is making.

   "They also tag turtles so they can use satellites to track their movements."

EXPAND YOUR KNOWLEDGE:
Even if you don't live near the ocean, you can still have a positive impact on sea turtles. To learn more about some of the things you can do, visit the following website:
www.defenders.org/sites/default/files/publications/five-things-you-can-do-to-save-sea-turtles.pdf

Cross out any extra words or phrases in the following sentences. If necessary, write in a word to replace them. Combine and rearrange sentences when you can. Choose more interesting and clear words to replace the underlined bolded words. You may need to consult a thesaurus. Write your revised sentences on the lines.

1. Sea turtles are **old** reptiles that live in the ocean. Sea turtles live in all of the world's oceans.

   _____

2. People use many parts of the turtles. Turtle shells are used to make jewelry. Using and selling things made from turtle parts is **against the law.**

   _____

   _____

3. Plastic product trash comes from the land. Plastic products wash out to sea in storm drains and rivers. Sea turtles mistake plastic **things** are food and are harmed.

   _____

   _____

4. Sea turtles are tagged. Tags help scientists follow sea turtle movement with satellites. Sea turtle movement shows where they nest and feed. This will help scientists decide where to **make** protected areas for sea turtle nesting.

   _____

   _____

   _____

Digging Deeper

Sea turtles face many threats in the oceans of the world. If you want to learn more about these threats and what is being done to help save sea turtles, visit the website at the following link to watch a video: *http://oceantoday.noaa.gov/endoceanseaturtles*

The Life Cycle of a Sea Turtle

1   Having lived on Earth for millions of years, sea turtles are among the most ancient creatures of our world. Like land turtles, a sea turtle's body is protected with an upper shell called a carapace (kare-uh-pace), but unlike land turtles, it can't hide its heads and legs inside this shell. Sea turtles walk slowly on land because their flippers are really made for swimming. Sea turtles spend most of their lives in the water and can travel long distances in the oceans, but they must come to the surface to breathe. A sea turtle's diet depends on what type of sea turtle it is. Some common foods they eat include jellyfish, seaweed, and crabs. Scientists think sea turtles can live up to seventy or eighty years! Currently, many of the sea turtle species are endangered, or at risk.

2   A sea turtle's life cycle begins when a female lays her eggs on a nesting beach. During nesting season, a female sea turtle will return to the same beach where she was born to lay her eggs. Depending on the species of turtle, she may lay somewhere between seventy to one-hundred-ninety soft-shelled eggs. It usually takes between six weeks to two months for the baby turtles to hatch.

3   Once the hatchlings are fully developed, they will break through their shells and surface from within their sandy nest. This usually happens at night so that the newly born sea turtles can use darkness to hide from predators and use the natural light of the moon to guide them to the ocean. Once in the water, baby turtles swim for several days to reach the open ocean. Because there are so many predators and dangers from human activity, few sea turtles live to adulthood.

4   After reaching the open ocean, sea turtles enter a stage that scientists sometimes call the "lost years," which might be as long as ten years. It is very hard to track their movements during this time because the turtles live away from shores to avoid predators that view them as food. When they finally return to more coastal waters, they are called juveniles and are about the size of dinner plates, which helps them avoid being eaten. They finish their growing period to adulthood near the coast where there is a larger variety and bigger supply of food.

5   Once sea turtles have reached adulthood, they travel to breeding and nesting grounds around the world. Many of these nesting grounds have been affected or destroyed by human activity. This journey can be anywhere from hundreds to thousands of miles. Most sea turtles will nest every two to four years over the course of their lifetimes. Many females return to nest at the very same beaches where they were born. Scientists are not sure how female turtles manage to find their way back, but they think the turtles use many clues, including ocean currents. Once reaching her birth beach, the female will dig a nest and lay her eggs, starting the process all over again.

COMPARING STRUCTURE

After reading "Saving the Sea Turtles" and "The Life Cycle of a Sea Turtle," compare the structure of the two articles and answer the question below.

1. Reread the first paragraphs of "Saving the Sea Turtles" and "The Life Cycle of a Sea Turtle." Answer the questions and put the information from the article into the graphic organizer below.

Which article's first paragraph is structured by compare and contrast? _____
_____

What is being compared and contrasted? _____
_____

What is similar? _____   What is different? _____
_____   _____

INFORMATION FROM VARIOUS SOURCES

Using the passages "Saving the Sea Turtles," "The Life Cycle of a Sea Turtle," and additional websites, answer the following questions.

1. In which article would the reader find information about how long a sea turtle lives? Why?

_____

_____

2. Which article would be **most** helpful to someone concerned with the extinction of sea turtles? How do you know?

_____

_____

3. Review the following websites:
    www.conserveturtles.org/seaturtleinformation.php?page=lighting
    www.sanibelseaschool.org/experience-blog/2014/6/4/5-ways-to-protect-sea-turtles

    How would you solve the problem artificial lighting presents to turtles? Give examples.

_____

_____

Use the passages "Saving the Sea Turtles," "The Life Cycle of a Sea Turtle," and the websites listed below to answer the following questions.

www.conserveturtles.org/seaturtleinformation.php?page=lighting
www.sanibelseaschool.org/experience-blog/2014/6/4/5-ways-to-protect-sea-turtles

1. What is the most interesting thing you learned about sea turtles from these passages?

_____

_____

2. List three common details found in both texts.

_____

_____

_____

3. What important details were discussed in "Saving the Sea Turtles" that were not discussed in "The Life Cycle of a Sea Turtle"?

_____

_____

_____

4. On a separate sheet of paper, draw a timeline of a sea turtle's life cycle. Mark the places on it where the sea turtle faces increased harm from manmade threats. Label each of these threats accordingly.

Digging Deeper

Sea turtles migrate great distances to feed and nest. If you want to know more about these turtle activities, visit the website at the following link to view two videos: *www.seeturtles.org/sea-turtle-life-cycle*

WRITE YOUR EXPLANATION

After reading "Saving the Sea Turtles" and "The Life Cycle of a Sea Turtle," use the expository organizer to plan a short, one-paragraph essay explaining how sea turtles are affected by human activity during their lives. *Hint:* You will need to choose an organizational structure for your text and focus on which activities you think pose risk to turtles.

Topic: _____

Organizational Structure: _____

Main Idea 1:	Main Idea 2:	Main Idea 3:

Supporting Detail:	Supporting Detail:	Supporting Detail:
_____	_____	_____
_____	_____	_____
_____	_____	_____
_____	_____	_____
_____	_____	_____

Summary Statement:

_____

_____

_____

Our Skies

How do you feel when you look up at our beautiful sky? What is your favorite thing to look at? A pretty sunset? Interesting cloud formations? A rainbow after a storm? In this unit, you will read about some amazing things that make our skies so beautiful.

Just Floating Around

Have you ever looked up in the sky to try to find elephant, dog, or ice cream shapes in the clouds? Cloud watching can be fun, but knowing more about the different types of clouds and how they formed can be even more interesting!

Types of Clouds

In general, there are three types of clouds: high, or "cirro," clouds; middle, or "alto," clouds; and low clouds. Clouds can form at any of these three levels in the sky and are identified by their shapes. We use the term "cumulus" when referring to a pile of clouds. Cumulus clouds look puffy like cotton. The term "stratus" refers to clouds that are long and streaky. The term "nimbus" refers to clouds that bring rain.

How Clouds Are Formed

Clouds are made of tiny water droplets or ice crystals that are suspended, or hanging, in the air. The four main ways that clouds can form are surface heating and cooling, the presence of mountains and other high **terrain**, air masses being forced to rise, and weather fronts.

I.   Warm air is able to hold more water than cool air. The warm air that is created when the sun heats the Earth can rise higher into the **atmosphere**. As it rises, it cools down and is no longer able to hold the water it was able to hold when it was warm. This water escapes or condenses out of the air and forms clouds. If the air near the Earth is cooler, clouds form closer to the ground or very high up in the sky. Eventually, if enough water condenses out of the air, water droplets will fall to Earth in the form of rain or snow.

II. A second way for clouds to form happens when air runs into a mountain range or other type of high land area. Again, the warm air rises, cools, and forms clouds.

III. A third way for clouds to form is when air masses are forced to rise. During high-pressure systems, air sinks, and in low-pressure systems, air rises. Wind moves in from all directions in a low-pressure system and causes the air to rise because it has nowhere else to go. Once again, clouds form when the warmer air rises and cools, allowing water droplets to condense, or escape, from the air.

IV.   A final way that clouds are formed has to do with weather fronts. Weather fronts occur when two large masses of air run into each other. Warm fronts make clouds when the warm air slides over the top of the cold air. Cold fronts make clouds when cold air forces warm air upward. If you think about it, all of these processes for cloud formation have something to do with the rising and cooling of warmer air and then the escaping of water from the air.

If you study the clouds long enough, you won't just be able to pick out the shapes of animals and objects. You just might be able to start predicting the weather!

After reading "Just Floating Around," answer the following questions.

1. Summarize the **two main ideas** of the passage in two sentences. Write your answer below.

_____

_____

2. Circle the sentence that contains the **best** supporting detail for one of the main ideas from the passage.

   A. Warm air rises, cools, and forms clouds.

   B. Knowing how clouds form can be interesting.

   C. There are several general types of clouds.

   D. Weather is determined by the air above our heads.

3. What can you **infer** about the weather in the presence of nimbostratus clouds? Support your answer with a quote from the text. Write your answer below.

_____

_____

_____

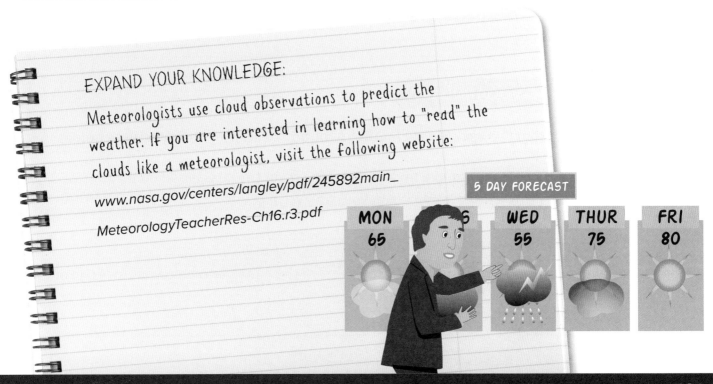

EXPAND YOUR KNOWLEDGE:

Meteorologists use cloud observations to predict the weather. If you are interested in learning how to "read" the clouds like a meteorologist, visit the following website:

www.nasa.gov/centers/langley/pdf/245892main_

MeteorologyTeacherRes-Ch16.r3.pdf

5 DAY FORECAST

MON		WED	THUR	FRI
65		55	75	80

After reading the text "Just Floating Around," answer the questions below.

Activity 1

1. What does it mean if *nimbo* appears at the beginning or *nimbus* appears at the end of a cloud name?

   A. It is a puffy cloud.   C. It is a high cloud.

   B. It is a wispy cloud.   D. It is a rain cloud.

2. What does it mean if *cumulo* appears at the beginning or *cumulus* appears at the end of a cloud name?

   A. It is a puffy cloud.   C. It is a rain cloud.

   B. It is a low cloud.   D. It is a curly cloud.

Use evidence from "Just Floating Around" to answer the questions below.

Activity 2

3. What are the characteristics of a **cirrostratus** cloud?

   _____

4. What are the characteristics of an **altocumulus** cloud?

   _____

UNDERSTANDING VOCABULARY

Use context clues from the text "Just Floating Around" to answer the questions below.

1. What does the term **atmosphere** mean? Use clues from the passage to help you understand what this word means. Write your answer below.

   _____

2. What does the term **terrain** mean? Use clues from the passage to help you understand what this word means. Write your answer below.

   _____

Northern Lights

1   Imagine a place where bright light streams across the sky in fantastic ribbons of color and dances delicately on the horizon. It's a light show that rivals firework displays and comes to you courtesy of nature. The **phenomenon** is called the aurora borealis (Uh-rohr-uh Bohr-ee-al-is), or northern lights, and takes place near the Earth's northern magnetic pole.

2   The aurora was originally named after the Roman goddess of dawn, and the term aurora borealis actually means "dawn of the north." It was thought that this special event was caused by sunlight reflected from polar snow and ice, in the same way sunlight reflects off water in the air to create rainbows. But now, scientists have a much better idea about what really causes the aurora borealis.

3   The northern lights are actually caused by energy particles, or small pieces of matter, from the sun colliding with, or running into, the Earth's invisible magnetic field. The surface of the sun is millions of degrees Fahrenheit. The gasses on the sun explode and collide with

each other, and some of the particles escape the sun's atmosphere. They are blown toward Earth on what is called a solar wind at about one million miles per hour. It takes these particles forty hours, or almost two days, to go from the sun to the Earth. The beautiful, bright lights, or the aurora, happen when the particles from the sun enter the Earth's magnetic field, or atmosphere. The Earth's magnetic atmosphere is weaker at the north and south poles, so that is where the sun particles usually manage to enter. This action mostly takes place between fifty and two hundred miles above Earth's surface.

4   The type of gas particle and the altitude at which it enters the Earth's magnetic field determine the color of light produced. Shades of greens and red are created by oxygen particles entering the Earth's magnetic field, while shades of blue and purple are created by nitrogen particles entering the Earth's magnetic field. Pale green and pink are the most common colors seen, while red is the rarest color. The lights that appear in the sky come in many forms. They might be scattered patches of light, streamers, rippling curtains, or shooting rays. All of these turn the sky into a beautiful, glowing light show.

5   It is easiest to see the northern lights at places closer to the North Pole, such as Canada, Alaska, Greenland, or the Arctic. In some of these locations, the northern lights are visible on most nights of the year. However, they are usually more spectacular from December to March. Surprisingly, the northern lights have been seen as far south as New Orleans in the western hemisphere!

6   People have been observing the northern lights since ancient times and wondering about them. Many cultural groups have legends that explain the lights. However, scientists now know that the gigantic light show that fills the sky comes from tiny particles from the sun entering the Earth's magnetic field. Even though we know what causes them, the northern lights are still mysterious and beautiful!

glossary

Phenomenon: a rare or significant fact or event

After reading "Northern Lights," complete the activity below.

1. Write a short summary of what you learned about the northern lights. Be sure to include the main ideas presented in the passage and specific details the author used to support those main ideas.

_____

_____

_____

_____

_____

_____

_____

_____

_____

_____

_____

_____

_____

_____

_____

Digging Deeper

If you would like to experience the Northern Lights yourself, you can view a time-lapse video of the Aurora Borealis set to music at the following link: _www.video.nationalgeographic.com/video/news/ norway-aurora- borealis-vin_

The three perfect tenses in the English language show action that has already been completed. In this case, the word perfect literally means made complete or completely done.

- The present perfect and the past perfect tenses are formed by the present or past tense of the verb *to have* + *the past participle* of a verb. (Past participles of verbs usually end in *–ed*, *-d*, *-t*, *-en*, or *–n*. Examples: swoll**en**, burn**t**, call**ed**)

- The future perfect is formed by an *auxiliary verb* + the present tense of the verb *to have* + the *past participle* of a verb. (The most common auxiliaries are forms of *be, can, do, may, must, ought, shall, will, has, have*, and *had*.)

Present Perfect: I **have seen** it. (Present tense of *to have* + *past participle* of *to see*. An action is completed in the present)

Past Perfect: I **had seen** it. (Past tense of *to have* + *past participle* of *to see*. An action is completed in the past)

Future Perfect: I **will have seen** it. (*Auxiliary verb* will + *present tense* of *to have* + *past participle* of *to see*. An action that is to be completed in the future.)

Example: Jimmy (to write) a letter.

Present perfect: Jimmy has written a letter.

Past perfect: Jimmy had written a letter.

Future perfect: Jimmy will have written a letter.

Use the verb provided in parentheses in each sentence to rewrite the sentence with each of the three verb tenses. You can refer to the list of auxiliaries above for help with the future perfect tense.

1. Some charged particles (to escape) the sun's atmosphere.

   Present perfect: _____.

   Past perfect: _____.

   Future perfect: _____.

2. It (to take) these particles forty hours to go from the Earth to the sun.

   Present perfect: _____.

   Past perfect: _____.

   Future perfect: _____.

3. The solar particles (to tear) through the Earth's magnetic field.

   Present perfect: _____.

   Past perfect: _____.

   Future perfect: _____.

WRITE YOUR NARRATIVE

Imagine that you are an explorer who has been sent on an expedition to the north by your country or community to investigate the eerie, mysterious lights that are glimpsed in the sky every now and then. You have finally arrived at your destination and have seen the full effect of the lights for the first time. Record your observations in your journal. Use a separate piece of paper to explain your experiences in more detail.

Hint: Remember to include details such as location, time of year, weather, and difficulties you encounter as well as sensory details involving sights and sounds.

Date:

Dear Journal,

REVIEW

Reading Fluency

Adults: Time your student for one minute while he or she reads. Make a note of where he or she is in the text after one minute to track fluency. Use the numbers on the right-hand margin to determine how many words have been read after one minute. Fifth graders should be able to read 120–150 words per minute. Have your student continue reading to the end of the passage to the questions that follow.

Wishing on a Star

Some people wish upon a star.	6
They think it will help them	12
reach their dreams. Do you think	18
this way?	20

You may know that a popular song spoke of this. People have been wishing and hoping 36
on shooting stars for a very long time. What might surprise you is that what we call 53
shooting stars or falling stars are not stars at all! Those amazing streaks of light that 69
flash across the sky are really caused by rocks and tiny, sand-sized grains of dust called 85
meteors that crash into Earth's atmosphere and burn up. As they burn up, they leave 100
incredible, bright flashes of light across the nighttime sky. If a meteor is big enough, 115
it might not burn all the way and may land on the Earth's surface. If it manages to land 134
 on the Earth, it is then called a meteorite. So far, about 38,000 meteorites have been 150
found on Earth. Most are found in hot deserts or in cold places such as Antarctica. 166

But where do meteors come from? Well, there are actually two explanations for the 180
shooting stars we see. Some of the meteors that fall into Earth's atmosphere are really 195
just bits of rock that have been smashed off from very large chunks of rock in outer space 213
called asteroids. Other shooting stars happen when Earth passes through the trails of gas 227
and dust a comet leaves behind as it orbits the sun. When this happens, it causes what is 245
called a meteor shower, and you can see as many as 100 shooting stars per hour! These 262

shooting stars are burning at about 30 to 40 miles above Earth's surface. There are   277
many comets that orbit our sun, so there are predictable times during the year when you   293
can watch meteor showers.   297

    If you go outside and watch the night sky long enough, you might be lucky enough to   314
spot shooting stars plunging through Earth's atmosphere. If you want to be like a real   329
astronomer, count the shooting stars and record your results. Also, never forget to wish   343
on one of those stars, too!   349

Words read in 1 minute — errors = WPM

REVISING SENTENCES

Combine and rearrange these sentences to create more complex sentence structures so the writing is not as choppy. You may have to cross out extra words or phrases and add words to replace them.

1. Falling stars are not really stars. Falling stars are rocks and dust that enter Earth's atmosphere. When falling stars enter the atmosphere, they burn up. This burning creates a streak of bright light in the sky.

    _____

    _____

    _____

2. If a meteor is big enough, it might not burn all the way. It may land on the Earth's surface. If it manages to land on the Earth, it is then called a meteorite. So far, about 38,000 meteorites have been found on Earth. Most are found in hot deserts or in cold places such as Antarctica.

    _____

    _____

    _____

3. Comets leave trails of gas and dust behind them. When Earth passes through the trails of gas and dust, it causes meteor showers. Sometimes you can see as many as 100 shooting stars per hour in a meteor shower.

    _____

    _____

    _____

VERB TENSE CONSISTENCY

Verb tense consistency means using the same verb tense within a sentence. All the verbs in a sentence should refer to the same time period, unless actions in the sentence happened at different times. Shifting verb tense in a sentence can confuse readers.

Example:
Incorrect: Gabe **read** a book and **plays** basketball.
Correct: Gabe **read** a book and **played** basketball.

Activity 1

Check the following sentences for shifts in verb tense. If the tense of each underlined verb construction is consistent or expresses the time relationship correctly, write C (for correct). If a shift in tense is not correct, write I (for incorrect) and make a change to one of the verbs. Keep in mind that sometimes there is more than one way to correct shifts in verb tense when revising sentences.

1. _____ What we **called** shooting stars or falling stars **are** not stars at all!

2. _____ When Earth **passes** through a comet trail, it **caused** a meteor shower.

3. _____ As they **burn** up, meteors **leave** bright streaks of light across the sky.

4. _____ Most meteorites that **have been found are** located in deserts or Antarctica.

5. _____ If a meteor **managed** to land, we would **call** it a meteorite.

Activity 2

Read these sentences below and underline the ones that contain incorrect verb tense shifts. Cross out the incorrect verb and write a correct verb above it.

Someday, I hope to be an astronomer who studies the stars. I am most interested in shooting stars and meteor showers because they told us a lot about the early formation of our solar system. One way scientists study them is to observe them when they come close to Earth. Another way to study them is by examining meteorites that landed on Earth's surface.

UNDERSTAND

Let's apply the reading skills you covered in this section.

After reading "Wishing on a Star," answer the following questions.

1. What does the word **orbit** mean? Use clues from the passage to help you determine the meaning.

_____

_____

2. Based on the passage "Wishing on a Star," what can you infer about comets?

_____

_____

3. Cite an example from the passage "Wishing on a Star" to support the **inference** you made in question 2. Remember to place quotation marks around any text you take directly from the passage when you write your answer.

_____

_____

4. What does the word **astronomer** mean? Use clues from the passage to help you determine the meaning.

_____

_____

5. Based on the passage "Wishing on a Star," what can you infer about astronomers?

_____

_____

6. Cite an example from the passage "Wishing on a Star" to support the inference you made in question 5. Remember to place quotation marks around any text you take directly from the passage when you write your answer on the following lines.

_____

_____

Standard RI.5.1, RI.5.3, RI.5.4

DISCOVER

What would you say? Let's take what you learned and write about it!

Write an Explanation

Imagine that you are a news reporter who has been assigned to write an article about an upcoming meteor shower for the newspaper. It is your job to provide the reading public with a good explanation of what they will be seeing in the nighttime sky. Remember to include information on the five Ws: who, what, when, where, and why.

Gathering Information:

Step 1: Reread the article "Wishing on a Star" on page 108.

Step 2: Ask an adult to help you search on the Internet for information. You will want to start by researching the schedule of meteor showers for this year.

> *Hint:* A good search engine to use is *www.google.com,* and you might use the phrase "meteor shower schedule" in your initial search.

Step 3: Choose one of the meteor showers to study, and search the Internet for one or two articles on that particular meteor shower. Try to choose the meteor shower that is the next one scheduled to occur.

> *Hint:* Again, *use www.google.com,* and this time, type in the name of the meteor shower you want to research.

Step 1: Read the articles you located and take some notes on the information you discover.

> *Hint:* Focus on information such as how the meteor shower got its name, what time of year it occurs, which comet causes it, and other interesting facts.

Starting to Write:

Step 5: Use the graphic organizer to arrange the information you found in your research.

Name of meteor shower
_____

Main Idea 1:
_____
_____
_____
_____

Supporting Details:
_____
_____
_____
_____
_____

Main Idea 2:
_____
_____
_____
_____

Supporting Details:
_____
_____
_____
_____
_____

Main Idea 3:
_____
_____
_____
_____

Supporting Details:
_____
_____
_____
_____
_____

Conclusion: _____
_____
_____

Step 6:   Take the information from your graphic organizer and write your explanation (main points and details) using complete sentences. Be sure to include transition words and phrases to link your ideas!

> **Transition words and phrases you might choose to use:**
>
> | for example | also | in fact | next | although |
> | for this reason | in addition | however | therefore | finally |
>
> *Remember to use a comma after transition words that begin sentences!*

Step 7:   Ask an adult to read what you have written. Work together to do the following:

• Make sure you have presented your opinion and two reasons clearly.

• Look for places where you can make better word choices.

• Proofread your paper for errors in grammar and punctuation.

• Pay special attention to commas with introductory elements and items in series.

Step 8:   With the help of an adult, contact your local community paper to see if they would be interested in publishing the article you have written. One way to submit the article is as a letter to the editor. The address and telephone number for your local community paper can usually be found online.

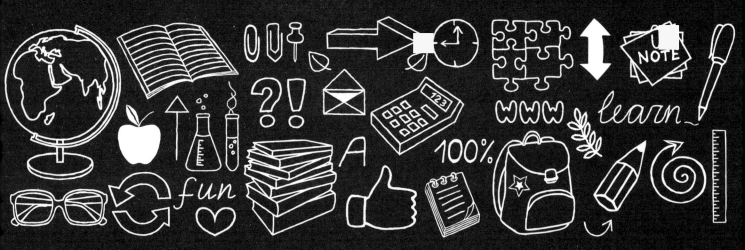

Reading and Writing: Literature

Tall Tales

Reading literature provides a look into an author's thoughts and feelings. It also reflects our world and the different ways that people behave with each other and with the world. Even though the material in this section is fictional, valuable life lessons can be learned. Literature can affect how a person thinks and feels, which in turn can shape the actions that a person may or may not choose to do.

Writing about literature will cause you to organize your thoughts and to clearly state what you think and feel. As you write, new discoveries in your thinking will create connections to ideas and concepts that you already know. Working through what at first may seem challenging will open new pathways of learning, understanding, and communicating.

While reading literature teaches you about other people, writing about literature teaches you about yourself!

In this unit you will read tall tales. These are traditional American stories about people who are larger than life. The main character, who is sometimes based on a real person, is usually bigger and stronger than a regular person. Also, the descriptions and events in tall tales are greatly exaggerated, or magnified. The main character of a tall tale often solves problems in ways that are humorous or hard to believe. Settlers who made their homes in the American wilderness were the first to tell these stories. People would gather in the evening after working all day and tell tall tales for entertainment. In this unit, you will read several tall tales and learn more about this traditional storytelling style.

Happy reading and writing!

John Henry: The Steel-Driving Man

A West Virginia Legend retold by S.E. Schlosser

1 Now John Henry was a mighty man, yes sir. He was born a slave in the 1840s but was freed after the war. He went to work as a steel-driver for the Chesapeake & Ohio Railroad, don't ya know. And John Henry was the strongest, the most powerful man working the rails.

2 John Henry, he would spend his days drilling holes by hitting thick steel spikes into rocks with his faithful shaker crouching close to the hole, turning the drill after each mighty blow. There was no one who could match him, though many tried.

3 Well, the new railroad was moving along right quick, thanks in no little part to the mighty John Henry. But looming right smack in its path was a mighty enemy—the Big Bend Mountain. Now the big bosses at the C&O Railroad decided that they couldn't go around the mile-and-a-quarter thick mountain. No sir, the men of the C&O were going to go through it—drilling right into the heart of the mountain.

4 A thousand men would lose their lives before the great enemy was conquered. It took three long years, and before it was done the ground outside the mountain was filled with **makeshift**, sandy graves. The new tunnels were filled with smoke and dust. Ya couldn't see no-how and could hardly breathe. But John Henry, he worked tirelessly, drilling with a fourteen-pound hammer, and going ten to twelve feet in one workday. No one else could match him.

5 Then one day a salesman came along to the camp. He had a steam-powered drill and claimed it could out-drill any man. Well, they set up a contest then and there between John Henry and that there drill. The **foreman** ran that **newfangled** steam-drill. John Henry, he just pulled out two twenty-pound hammers, one in each hand. They drilled and drilled, dust rising everywhere. The men were howling and cheering. At the end of thirty-five minutes, John Henry had drilled two seven-foot holes—a total of fourteen feet, while the steam drill had only drilled one nine-foot hole.

6   John Henry held up his hammers in triumph! The men shouted and cheered. The noise was so loud, it took a moment for the men to realize that John Henry was tottering. Exhausted, the mighty man crashed to the ground, the hammers rolling from his grasp. The crowd went silent as the foreman rushed to his side. But it was too late. A blood vessel had burst in his brain. The greatest driller in the C&O Railroad was dead. Some folks say that John Henry's likeness is carved right into the rock inside the Big Bend Tunnel. And if you walk to the edge of the blackness of the tunnel, sometimes you can hear the sound of two twenty-pound hammers drilling their way to victory over the machine.

glossary

Foreman: A person in charge of a group of workers
Makeshift: A temporary substitute
Newfangled: Of a new kind or fashion

After reading "John Henry: The Steel-Driving Man," answer the questions below.

1. Which of the following statements best reflects the **theme** of the story?

   A. John Henry was a big and strong man.

   B. Human workers should be valued more than machines.

   C. The digging of the Big Bend Mountain tunnel.

   D. John Henry died because of a competition with a steam drill.

2. How did the characters in the story solve the **conflict**?

   A. John Henry decided to dig through Big Bend Mountain.

   B. John Henry competed against the steam drill.

   C. John Henry escaped slavery and worked for the railroad.

   D. The characters cheered John Henry to victory.

3. Find an example from the story to support the answer you provided for question 2. Remember to use quotation marks if you take material directly from the text.

_____

_____

_____

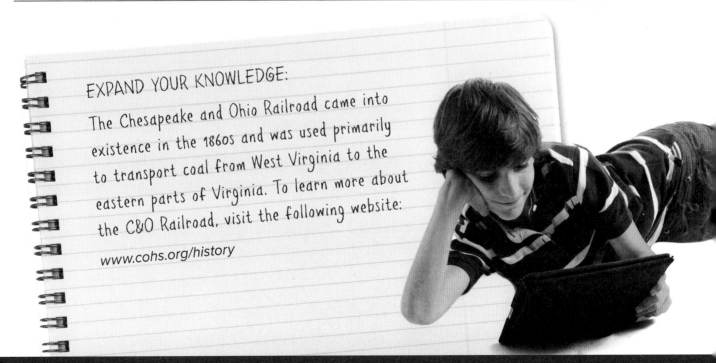

EXPAND YOUR KNOWLEDGE:

The Chesapeake and Ohio Railroad came into existence in the 1860s and was used primarily to transport coal from West Virginia to the eastern parts of Virginia. To learn more about the C&O Railroad, visit the following website:

www.cohs.org/history

After reading "John Henry: The Steel-Driving Man," answer the following questions.

Explain why each of the following sentences from the story could be considered examples of hyperbole.

1. *"A thousand men would lose their lives before the great enemy was conquered."*

_____

_____

_____

2. *"At the end of thirty-five minutes, John Henry had drilled two seven-foot holes—a total of fourteen feet, while the steam drill had only drilled one nine-foot hole."*

_____

_____

_____

Challenge: Add hyperboles to this paragraph about John Henry. Replace all of the words in parenthesis with a hyperbole that indicates the same meaning but is a big exaggeration.

Write your hyperboles on the lines provided.

On the night John Henry was born lightning (**struck**) _____ in

the sky and thunder (**rumbled**) _____ . Just after he was born,

John Henry was hungry and asked his mother for (**a meal**) _____

_____ . When he did not get enough to eat, he got angry and

(**threw things**) _____ . After that,

everyone knew not to mess around when Baby John was hungry!

ANALYZING MEDIA

Below Left: Steel drivers worked in teams to dig railroad tunnels through mountains. A steel driver used a long-handled hammer to pound a steel spike into the rock. A "shaker" would hold the spike in place, continuously turning it, while the steel driver hammered it. Then a blaster would pack explosives into the hole. This would blast big sections of the rock away.

Below Right: By the 1860s, mechanical rock drills designed to do the jobs of the steel driver and shaker teams gained in popularity. The Burleigh compressed air steam drill (pictured below) was one of these rock drills. It could drill many holes at one time.

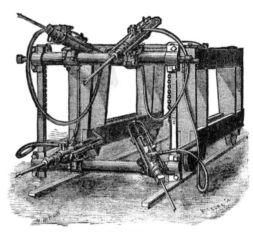

FIG. 102.
BURLEIGH FOUR-DRILL CARRIAGE.

The Great Bend Tunnel is the place where the tale of John Henry's contest with the steam drill is supposed to have taken place. Watch the video to learn more about it here: *www.wvencyclopedia.org/articles/2154*

After reviewing the images and the video cited above, answer the following questions about "John Henry: The Steel-Driving Man."

1. How do the pictures help you to understand who John Henry was?

_____

_____

2. How does the video support the tone of the story of "John Henry: The Steel-Driving Man?"

_____

_____

Pecos Bill Rides a Tornado

A Kansas Tall Tale retold by S.E. Schlosser

1 Now everyone in the West knows that Pecos Bill could ride anything. No bronco could throw him, no sir! Fact is, I only heard of Bill gettin' throwed once in his whole career as a cowboy.

2 Yep, it was that time he was up Kansas way and decided to ride him a tornado.

3 Now Bill wasn't gonna ride jest any tornado, no ma'am. He waited for the biggest gol-durned tornado you ever saw. It was turning the sky black and green and roaring so loud it woke up the farmers away over in China. Well, Bill jest grabbed that there tornado, pushed it to the ground, and jumped on its back. The tornado whipped and whirled and sidewinded and generally cussed its bad luck all the way down to Texas. Tied the rivers into knots, flattened all the forests so bad they had to rename one place the Staked Plains. But Bill jest rode along all calm-like, give it an occasional jab with his spurs.

4 Finally, that tornado decided it wasn't getting this cowboy off its back no-how. So it headed west to California and jest rained itself out. Made so much water it washed out the Grand Canyon. That tornado was down to practically nothing when Bill finally fell off. It hit the ground so hard it sank below sea level. Folks call the spot Death Valley.

5 Anyway, that's how rodeo got started. Though most cowboys stick to broncos these days.

EXPAND YOUR KNOWLEDGE:
The sport known as rodeo grew from the cattle industry in the American West. The early roots of the sport go all the way back to the 1500s! To learn more about the history of rodeo, visit the following website:
www.tshaonline.org/handbook/online/articles/llr01

DRAWING CONCLUSIONS

After reading "Pecos Bill Rides a Tornado," answer the questions below.

1. List one **inference,** or conclusion, that you can make about Pecos Bill based on the story.

_____

_____

_____

2. Use a quote from the story to support the answer you provided for question 1.

_____

_____

_____

Digging Deeper

Calf-roping is a skill used by actual cowboys to catch calves. Cowboys took pride in the speed with which they caught calves with a rope. Today, people still carry on the tradition of calf-roping in rodeos. None of the calves are harmed in calf-roping. To learn more about calf-roping, view the video at this website: _http://video.pbs.org/video/2365234815_

UNDERSTANDING VERBS

Understanding the different verb tenses and how to correctly use them makes you better writers.

- Verb tenses are used to convey various times and sequences in which actions occur. Generally, you think of them as *past*, *present*, and *future* tenses.

> **Example:** I walked (past), I walk (present), and I will walk (future)

- The **progressive tense** is another verb tense that involves action that *is*, *was*, or *will be* in progress at a certain time.
- Progressive tense verbs are formed with a "be" verb + -*ing*

> **Examples:** I was learning to play the cello (past progressive)
> I am learning to play the cello (present progressive)
> I will be learning to play the cello (future progressive)

Activity 1

Indicate which progressive verb tense is used in each of the following sentences. Write your answers on the lines provided.

1. Pecos Bill was riding a tornado across the west. _____

2. Next summer, I will be seeing the spot called Death Valley, where Pecos Bill fell off the tornado. _____

3. My brother, a rodeo rider, is following all the rules of bronco riding so he can become famous like Pecos Bill! _____

Activity 2

Write a sentence about the rodeo using each of the progressive tenses of the verb *to watch*.

1. Past progressive: _____

   _____

2. Present progressive: _____

   _____

3. Future Progressive: _____

   _____

Standard L.5.1.c

COMPARING VARIETIES OF ENGLISH DIALECTS

- Dialects are forms of language that are specific to groups of people or to regions of countries.
- Using dialect allows the writer to convey information about the time, setting, and characters without adding extra words and descriptions. It makes the story genuine, or honest, and believable. It can also show differences between characters.

Examples:
Howdy y'all! ⟶ Hello, everyone!
I'm fixin' to go to the store ⟶ I am preparing to go to the store.

After reading "Pecos Bill Rides a Tornado," answer the questions below.

1. Based on the language the narrator of "Pecos Bill Rides a Tornado" uses, from what region of the country do you think he or she comes? What makes you think that?

_____

_____

_____

2. Why do you think the author used this specific dialect in the story?

_____

_____

3. Pick two instances where a dialect other than Standard English is used in the story. Write the sentence as it appears in the story. Then, rewrite the sentence by replacing the dialect with Standard English.

Examples:
I only heard of Bill gettin' throwed once.
I only heard of Bill getting thrown once.

A._____

_____

B._____

_____

Tales of Paul Bunyan

1   The birth of Paul Bunyan was all the folks of Bangor, Maine, could talk about when he first arrived. After all, it had taken five giant storks just to deliver him to his parents! Baby Paul was so huge that they had to use a lumber wagon for his bed. They used a whole team of horses tied to this lumber wagon to walk up and down a mountain just to rock baby Paul to sleep! His parents could barely keep up with feeding him, and when baby Paul was hungry, his stomach rumbled like thunder. In fact, when he got hungry, his cries were as loud as train whistles! One holler from Baby Paul could empty a whole river of fish! When he was just a few weeks old, Paul rolled around too much during his nap. He ruined four square miles of forest as the trees snapped like matchsticks under his weight. After this, his parents decided it might be better to use a raft for his crib. They had a giant one built for this purpose and floated it in the Bay of Fundy off the coast of Maine. This didn't work either because when Paul rolled over, it just caused tidal waves! One tidal wave was so huge it sank four ships!

2   Now, even though Paul Bunyan's parents stuck with him through thick and thin, they knew their son needed more elbow room than what the state of Maine could provide. So, they took the bull by the horns and left their neck of the woods to search for a new place to live. They ended up paying an arm and a leg for a new house and land in Minnesota. Their neighbors were few and far between, and Paul had no playmates. So, his parents gave him a pet blue ox named Babe for his first birthday. Paul and Babe were a great fit and became the very best of friends. Babe was just as big as Paul and ate as much as thirty bales of hay for just a snack!

3   Over the years, Paul and Babe had many great adventures together. It is said that the tracks they made in the mud and dirt as they played tag and hide and go seek all around Minnesota eventually filled up with water. Now Minnesota is known as the land of 10,000 lakes! As the two friends got older, Babe began traveling the country and helping Paul at his job as a lumberjack.

4   One day, Paul was as tired as a worn out shoe after working all day long. Instead of holding his big ax up on his shoulder as he usually did, Paul dragged it behind him on the ground. That heavy ax cut through the dirt as if it was butter. When Paul finally looked around, he exclaimed to Babe, "My, what a grand canyon!" Well, the name stuck like glue! That's how and why we now have the Grand Canyon in Arizona!

DETERMINING THEMES

The conflict in a piece of literature is the central problem in the text. Every storyline involves some kind of conflict or struggle between two forces. It is important for you to be able to identify the conflict in order to fully understand the story.

After reading "Tales of Paul Bunyan," answer the questions below.

1. What is the **central problem** or challenge in this story?

_____

_____

_____

_____

_____

2. How do the characters in the story solve the problem or meet the **challenge**?

_____

_____

_____

_____

_____

3. Write a short two- or three-sentence summary of the article.

_____

_____

_____

_____

_____

_____

_____

A simile is a type of figurative language that compares two unlike things using the words *like* or *as*.

> Examples: The baby had **a smile as sweet as sugar**.
>   Traffic **crawled like a snail**.

Circle the simile in each sentence. In the space provided, explain what two things are being compared.

1. When Paul Bunyan rolled over in his sleep, the trees snapped like twigs.

    _____ is being compared to _____

2. Paul Bunyan's alarm clock really is as loud as cannon fire!

    _____ is being compared to _____

3. When baby Paul was hungry his stomach rumbled like thunder.

    _____ is being compared to _____

4. Baby Paul's cries were as loud as train whistles.

    _____ is being compared to _____

UNDERSTANDING IDIOMS

Idioms are common words, phrases, and expressions that cannot be taken literally. They are an important part of every language, and every language has its own unique idioms.

> Examples: *It's raining cats and dogs* does not mean dogs and cats are falling from the sky!
>   It is an expression that means it is raining very heavily.

List two examples of idioms from the story. Explain what each means.

A. _____

_____

B. _____

_____

Challenge: Some common idioms in language are actually also examples of similes. Can you think of at least two idioms that are also similes? Write your answers on the lines provided.

> ### Example: She is as busy as a bee.

_____

_____

REVISING SENTENCES

Revise the sentences in this passage by combining choppy sentences and including your own similes in place of the underlined descriptions so that they are more expressive and interesting for readers. Rewrite your new sentences on the lines provided.

Paul Bunyan was <u>very large</u>. He was also <u>super strong</u>. Not only was Paul Bunyan strong, but he was <u>extremely tall</u>. Given his size, it's a good thing that he tried to be <u>gentle</u> in the things he did. It seemed the only thing he never managed to control was his booming voice. He was <u>very loud</u> all the time.

_____

_____

_____

_____

_____

_____

_____

_____

_____

Now you get the chance to be a folklorist by writing your very own tall tale! You will need to be creative and develop a character, a setting, a conflict, and a solution to the conflict. Use the graphic organizer below to get you started.

Main Character: Be sure to use hyperbole to describe your character!

List of character traits:

You may choose to begin your tall tale like this:

_____ was the (tallest, wisest, strongest, etc.) in the entire

state of _____ .

Conflict: Describe the problem in the story.

You can begin to explain the conflict like this:

One day, (name of character) went / saw / stumbled upon / heard

_____ and decided to _____ .

Important Events: Describe what happened when the main character took action.

You can begin to explain the main events like this:

Luckily, (name of character) knew what to do. He /she _____ .*

*Remember to use transition words like _first, second, next, and after that._

Resolution: Tell how the problem was finally solved and what the final outcome was.

You can begin to explain the resolution like this:

In the end, (name of character) was able to _____ .

Myths

A myth is a traditional story that teaches a lesson, tells why something happened, or explains the unexplainable in a way for people to understand. Myths use supernatural characters or events. Myths were shared by groups of people and over time became part of their culture. The word "myth" comes from the Greek word "mythos," which means "word of mouth." In this unit, you will learn about some myths from different cultures and discover how they have been used to explain events and interesting happenings in nature.

Why the Possum's Tail Is Bare

A Cherokee Myth

1 The Possum used to have a long, bushy tail and was so proud of it that he combed it out every morning and sang about it at the dance, until the Rabbit, who had had no tail since the Bear pulled it out, became very jealous and made up his mind to play a trick on the Possum.

2 There was to be a great **council** and a dance at which all the animals were to be present. It was the Rabbit's business to send out the news, so as he was passing the Possum's place, he stopped to ask him if he intended to be there. The Possum said he would come if he could have a special seat, "because I have such a handsome tail that I ought to sit where everybody can see me." The Rabbit promised to attend to it and also to send someone to comb and dress the Possum's tail for the dance. The Possum was very much pleased and agreed to come.

3   Then the Rabbit went over to the Cricket, who was such an expert hair cutter that the Indians called him the barber, and told him to go the next morning and dress the Possum's tail for the dance that night. He told the Cricket just what to do and then went on about some other mischief.

4   In the morning the Cricket went to the Possum's house and said he had come to get him ready for the dance. So the Possum stretched himself out and shut his eyes while the Cricket combed out his tail and wrapped a red string around it to keep it smooth until night. But all this time, as Cricket wound the string around, he was clipping off the hair close to the roots, and the Possum never knew it.

5   When it was night, the Possum went to the townhouse where the dance was to be and found the best seat ready for him, just as the Rabbit had promised. When his turn came in the dance he loosened the string from his tail and stepped into the middle of the floor. The drummers began to drum and the Possum began to sing, "See my beautiful tail." Everybody shouted and he danced around the circle and sang again, "See what a fine color it has." They shouted again and he danced around another time, singing, "See how it sweeps the ground." The animals shouted more loudly than ever, and the Possum was delighted. He danced around again and sang, "See how fine the fur is." Then everybody laughed so long that the Possum wondered what they meant. He looked around the circle of animals and they were all laughing at him. Then he looked down at his beautiful tail and saw that there was not a hair left upon it, but that it was as bare as the tail of a lizard. He was so astonished and ashamed that he could not say a word, but rolled over helpless on the ground and grinned, as the Possum does to this day when taken by surprise.

glossary

Council: An assembly or meeting for advice or discussion

- The theme is a message about people or life that the author wants the reader to understand. The theme is usually not stated directly in a story, and the reader must infer or figure out what the theme is. Theme is expressed as a complete thought (sentence).

- An easy way to remember that theme is about the message is to remember that the words "the message" begin with theme ···▹ **The me**ssage.

After reading "Why the Possum's Tail Is Bare," answer the questions below.

1. Which of the following statements best reflects the theme of the story?
   A. Beauty is more important than anything else.
   B. Being proud and boastful is not a good way to behave.
   C. Playing tricks is not a good way to solve problems.
   D. Differences should be admired and valued.

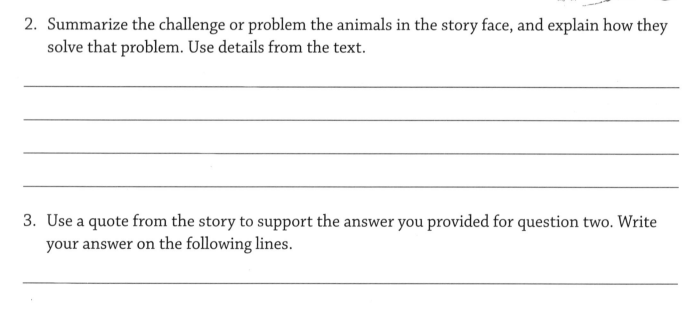

2. Summarize the challenge or problem the animals in the story face, and explain how they solve that problem. Use details from the text.

_____

_____

_____

_____

3. Use a quote from the story to support the answer you provided for question two. Write your answer on the following lines.

_____

_____

Digging Deeper

"Why the Possum's Tail Is Bare" was adapted and produced for Native Radio Theater by Kevin Norris, Shawn Crowe, and the Cherokee High School Theatre Arts Class. You can listen to this performance at the following website: *www.learnnc.org/lp/editions/nc-american- indians/5995*

PREPOSITIONS

- A preposition is a part of speech that shows a relationship, such as location, timing, or direction, between two things.

- Common prepositions are: *on, under, in, below, before, after, until, from, off.*

- They **always** appear in prepositional phrases. Prepositional phrases function as adjectives or adverbs in sentences.

- As adjectives, prepositional phrases answer the question *Which one?*

- As adverbs, prepositional phrases answer the questions such as *How?, When?,* or *Where?*

Examples: The squirrel **in** the tree is brown. (Answers *Which squirrel?* – adj.)
Before class, I returned my library book. (Answers *When?* – adv.)

Example: We cheered **during** the football game. ⤏ adv. – Answers *When?*

Identify whether the bolded preposition functions as an adverb or an adjective in each of the following sentences. Then explain what question it answers.

1. **In** the morning, the Cricket went to the Possum's house. _____

2. Possum loosened the string **from** his tail. _____

3. The dance **in** the townhouse was attended by all the animals. _____

4. Possum twirled **around** the dance floor and sang. _____

5. All the animals laughed **with** glee. _____

6. **At** that moment, Possum had been surprised. _____

7. There was not a hair left **upon** his tail. _____

How the Chipmunk Got Its Stripes

An Iroquois Myth

1   Many, many moons ago, Earth was blanketed in darkness. None of the woodland creatures had ever seen the sun and lived in constant darkness.

2   One day, all of the forest animals gathered for a meeting in the meadow. Some of the animals suggested that it might be good to have light instead of always living in the dark. That evening, Deer, Chipmunk, Raccoon, Wolf, Bear, and the other animals climbed the mountain to the very top. From there, they could see millions of stars glittering in the sky. It was a beautiful sight. Bear, being the most powerful animal in all of the forest, spoke first. He told the others that it would be best to remain in darkness because that is how they were used to living, and the light would only cause problems such as keeping them awake when they tried to sleep.

3   Since most of the other animals were afraid of Bear, they agreed with him so that he would not become angry. Wolf said that she did not mind the darkness at all, for it was just as easy to howl in the darkness as it was to howl in the light. Raccoon agreed and said that he did not mind the darkness either because it was just as easy for him to find food in the dark as it would be to find food in the light. All of the animals were afraid to say what they really thought. But not Chipmunk! Even though she was the smallest of all the creatures, she was the only one brave enough to stand up to the powerful bear. Chipmunk argued that it would be better to have both darkness and light. Bear, of course, completely disagreed. He continued to argue for darkness, while Chipmunk argued for light.

4   Now, Chipmunk was very clever, you see, and she continued to argue for many hours. Eventually, Bear himself grew weary and stopped talking. But not Chipmunk! She had a lot of energy and chattered on for hours about how wonderful it would be to have light. Slowly, but surely, all of the animals began to fall asleep. But not Chipmunk! She kept chattering away! Slowly, the night slipped away, and tiny pink and gold rays appeared on the horizon. The sun began to lift its head over the top of the mountain. All of the forest animals awoke one by one and were amazed by what they saw. It was the very first sunrise!

5   Chipmunk had outsmarted Bear and began dancing with glee from rock to rock. This angered Bear because he was used to getting his own way all the time. All of the other animals shrank back in fear because an angry bear was never a good thing. But not Chipmunk! She stood her ground and teased Bear about how she had outsmarted him. Bear became very angry and let out his mighty roar. He began to chase Chipmunk all over the mountain top and down the side of the mountain. Chipmunk darted this way and that and almost got away. But Bear was really fast and managed to take a swipe at Chipmunk with his big, powerful paw just before she reached the entrance to her home. His long, sharp claws scratched down Chipmunk's back just as she went into her hole. From that day forward, every Chipmunk ever born has had stripes down its back to pay honor to the battle with Bear over the very first sunrise.

In this unit, you've already read two stories. Since both stories are myths, they probably have many similarities. They also may have some differences. When analyzing two stories in the same genre, think about how the author discusses similar topics or themes. Are the main characters the same? How are they different? Exploring and comparing these relationships and patterns helps make sense of the information in the stories.

After reading "Why the Possum's Tail Is Bare" and "How the Chipmunk Got Its Stripes," answer the following questions.

1. Why did early people tell stories like myths? Use evidence from the text to support your answer.

   _____

   _____

2. How are the characters in both myths the same?

   _____

   _____

3. How are the settings in the two myths different?

   _____

   _____

4. Using the chart below, list the similarities between the two stories. Then, tell what is different about each story.

Why the Possum's Tail Is Bare	Both Myths	How the Chipmunk Got Its Stripes

5. List one small difference in the way these two myths are written.

_____

_____

_____

_____

_____

_____

INTERJECTIONS

- An interjection is a word that is added to a sentence to convey emotion, such as surprise, disgust, or excitement, or to show sounds.
- They often appear at the beginning of a sentence (but not always).
- They are followed by either an exclamation point for expressing stronger emotion or a comma for expressing milder emotion.

> **Commonly Used Interjections:**
>
> alas, aww, aha, gee, great, ha, hooray, hey, huh, no, oh, oops, ouch, phew, um, well, wow, yes, yikes, yippee, yuck

Underline the interjection in each of the following sentences. Based on the level of emotion expressed in the sentence, decide whether to punctuate it with a comma or an exclamation point.

1. Gee Chipmunk sure does look pretty with those new stripes.

2. Hooray we will now have a sunrise every morning!

3. No I don't think Bear is very pleased about the situation.

4. Wow Bear sure did get angry at Chipmunk!

5. Ouch I bet it really hurt when Bear took a swipe at Chipmunk!

6. Phew I am glad Chipmunk will be ok.

7. Well I do think that Bear should at least apologize to Chipmunk.

Challenge: Write your own sentence using an interjection.

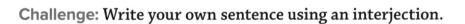

_____

_____

_____

Even in the age of computer programs that check spelling, it is important to learn how to correctly spell words on your own. Learning how to accurately spell words not only helps you become a better writer, but it also encourages good reading skills.

One word in each of the following sentences is misspelled. Write the word correctly on the line provided. Then, use a dictionary or glossary to check your work.

1. The animals had gone to the top of the mountain to make a desision on whether or not they needed light.

   _____

2. Bear grew very inpatient with Chipmunk as she continued to argue in favor of daylight.

   _____

3. None of the other animals would even attept to argue with Bear.

   _____

4. Clearly, Chipmunk was quit brave to stand up to Bear with her opinion.

   _____

5. Some of the animals agreed with Chipmunk's excllent idea even though they were afraid to say anything.

   _____

6. Chipmunk displayed a lot of patiens by continuing to make her point as all the others became sleepy and started dozing off.

   _____

7. When the sunrise came fourth, all of the animals were amazed at its beauty.

   _____

8. Bear was fuious after the sun rose because he did not get his way.

   _____

9. Most everyone agreed that Bear had acted in a rediculus way and wanted him to apologize to Chipmunk.

   _____

10. Thankfully, Bear did apologize, and he and Chipmunk are freinds once again.

   _____

Crow Brings Daylight

An Inuit Myth

1   At the very beginning of time when the Earth was brand new, the Inuit people of the north lived in complete darkness. They ate in the dark, hunted in the dark, celebrated in the dark, and slept in the dark. It was Crow who first explained to them what daylight was, for you see, he had seen the light on his many journeys south. At first, the **Inuit** did not believe Crow, with his magnificent descriptions of the sparkling light. However, they eventually started thinking that maybe they, too, would like to live in a world of light instead of one covered in drab shadows. They made Crow repeat his tales of the land to the south that was covered in brilliant light. Finally, they became desperate and begged him to bring some light to them.

2   "No," he told them. "The land of daylight is so very far away, and I am too old to fly that far."

3   Eventually, the Inuit convinced Crow to make the journey to the south and retrieve some light for them. Crow flew through the vast north, which was covered in an endless, black

blanket. Just as Crow was about to turn back, for the journey truly was hard on his old wings, a rim of brilliant light appeared on the horizon bringing a warmth to his old, aching bones. Suddenly, Crow was filled with purpose. He flapped his old wings with all his might until the daylight exploded upon him in a shower of brilliance. Though he had seen these sights before, the beautiful colors and shapes of the lighted world took his breath away.

4   Crow rested a while and then made his way to a local village sat alongside a rippling river that sparkled in the sunshine. He carefully made his way to the head chief's lodge and peered inside the door. There, Crow spied a box tied with string that glimmered and glowed around its edges.

5   "It's the secret of the sacred daylight!" thought Crow. "They will never give it up willingly, so I will need to come up with a plan."

6   It was then that Crow noticed a small boy sitting on the floor. Cleverly, Crow distracted the chief by making the little boy cry. When the chief had his back turned, Crow swooped in and snatched the glowing box of daylight by the string that held it closed. The box fell open, but Crow held fast to the string and flapped his wings harder than he ever had before. He disappeared into the beautiful blue sky filled with puffy white clouds with the ball of glowing daylight trailing behind him on a string.

7   Eventually, the Inuit of the north saw the approach of Crow, for there were rays of light ripping through the darkness. When Crow arrived, he let go of the string, and the ball shattered into a million pieces as it hit the Earth. Brilliant light skipped and scattered everywhere! The mountains, valleys, and rivers came alive with light. Sun gleamed and sparkled across the snow and ice and made the colors of the land dance with brilliance! The Inuit cried with joy at the sight of their world filled with light. It was then that Crow explained that daylight would not last, for he had only taken one ball of light from the people of the south. The light would only last for six months before it would need to rest and regain its strength to return again. To this day, the Inuit of the north have daylight for half the year and darkness for the other half.

glossary

Inuit: A member of a group of native people of northern North America and Greenland

After reading "Crow Brings Daylight," answer the questions below.

1. List some details that describe the setting in the north before Crow brought the daylight and after Crow brought the daylight.

Before	After

2. Which statement best describes how Crow treats the people of the North compared to the way he treats the people of the South? Circle the letter of the correct answer.

A. Crow was rude to those in the North and kind to those in the South.

B. Crow was disrespectful to those in the North and secretive with those in the South.

C. Crow was kind to those in the North and disrespectful to those in the South.

D. Crow was sneaky toward those in the North and secretive with those in the South

EXPAND YOUR KNOWLEDGE:

The Inuit are a cultural group of people who live in the Arctic regions of the United States, Canada, and Greenland. In the U.S., they live in Alaska and are often called Eskimos. In Alaska, the day and night are very different than what they are in the rest of the country. In the northernmost parts of Alaska, there is no sunlight for 64 days in the winter! You can learn more about it at the following website:

http://alaska.gov/kids/learn/daylighthours.htm

IMAGERY

Imagery is a form of figurative language and is made up of the words and phrases writers use to appeal to the reader's senses (sight, sound, taste, touch, and smell).

Writers use colorful descriptions to do the following things:

- Create mental pictures for the reader
- Stir feelings in the reader
- Create moods in their writing

Here are some examples that illustrate what a difference the use of imagery can make in writing.

Examples: The pavement was hot. ⟶ Heat rose in waves from the scorching hot pavement.

The alarm clock went off. ⟶ The piercing, shrill beeping of the alarm clock ripped through the peaceful morning air.

After reading "Crow Brings Daylight," answer the questions below.

1. Read the following line from the story.

   "Just as Crow was about to turn back, for the journey truly was hard on his old wings, a rim of brilliant light appeared on the horizon bringing a warmth to his old, aching bones."

   To which of the five senses does this image appeal?_____

   What do you think the author is describing with this image? Explain your answer.

   _____

   _____

2. Read the following lines from the story.

   "He disappeared into the beautiful blue sky filled with puffy white clouds, with the ball of glowing daylight trailing behind him on a string."

   To which of the five senses does this image appeal? _____

   What do you think the author is describing with this image? Explain your answer.

   _____

   _____

REVIEW

Reading Fluency

Adults: While your student is reading, time him or her for one minute and mark any words that were missed by writing the word or crossing it out. When you get to one minute, note where your student has stopped, but allow him or her to continue the story. Fifth graders should be able to read 120–150 words per minute. Count the total number of errors and subtract that from the number of words read. This will give you the total number of words read per minute.

When Badger Named the Sun

At the beginning of the era of the Surem,	9
nobody knew the name of the sun and they wanted	19
a name for it. For this reason, they held a council	30
on the bank of the Surem river. Everyone gave	39
his opinion, but no name was found for the sun.	49
Every day they studied the matter. They did	57
not know if it were man or woman and so they	68
couldn't decide whether it would be best to give	77
it a male or a female name. The Surem could not	88

agree. They finally invited all the animals of the world to come to a council. 103

Once they were all present, before the sun came up, at the edge of the river, they made a 122
great group of men and animals. When the sun appeared, a badger came out of a hole where 140
he lived in the ground. The badger came to the council and said in a strong voice, "The sun 159
being a man, comes out of a hole in the Earth as I do." Speaking thus, he ran away. 178
Everyone ran after him, wishing to pay him honor for his great intelligence. They wanted 193
to give a fiesta for him and to pay him well with abundant food. But the badger ran away and 213
went into his hole and would not come out. He thought they wanted to punish him. From that 231
time on the badger rarely goes out on the plains. He is still afraid that they might punish him 250
for something. 252

Words read in 1 minute – errors = WPM

After reading "When Badger Named the Sun," answer the following questions.

1. Why do writers use interjections? Write your answer on the line.

_____

_____

_____

2. Underline the interjections in the following passage. Punctuate the interjection using a comma or exclamation point (based on level of emotion). Capitalize the next sentence if using an exclamation point.

Hooray the badger has told us the sun is a male so that we can choose a perfect name! Wow he must be so proud of himself for being so smart. Yikes where is he going? Aww he thinks we are angry with him. Gee that's too bad.

3. Circle each misspelled word in the following passage. Correctly spell each of the words on the lines below. There are a total of seven misspelled words.

The badger informed us that the sun was male so that we could choose a name. Afterword, he ran away and hid. We wanted to give him credet for helping us. We thought he was just being humbel when he made the desision to hide. But that was not the case. He really was in destress and would not buge from his hole. No matter what we did, we could not convinse him to come out.

_____

_____

_____

UNDERSTAND

After reading "When Badger Named the Sun," answer the questions below.

1. What was **the conflict** in the story?

   A. The animals and men wished to honor the badger.

   B. The badger stayed in his hole because he feared punishment.

   C. No one knew the name of the sun and wanted to name it.

   D. The badger told the council the sun was a man.

2. Use examples from the story to support the answer you provided for question 1.

   _____

   _____

   _____

3. How was the conflict in the story resolved? List evidence from the text.

   _____

   _____

   _____

4. What does "When Badger Named the Sun" explain or teach?

   _____

   _____

   _____

   _____

   _____

   _____

DISCOVER

What would you say? Let's take what you learned and write about it!

Write Your Narrative

Imagine that you are among the earliest people on earth. Many things in your world need names and need to be explained. For instance, why does the moon glow in the night sky? Why does the cat meow? Why do turtles hide their heads, arms, and legs in their shells? Why does it thunder? It is your job to write a myth to explain some event or thing in your community.

Gathering Information:

Step 1:   Reread the myths "Why the Possum's Tail Is Bare," "How the Chipmunk Got Its Stripes," and "Crow Brings Daylight."

Step 2:   Choose an event or characteristic of something to explain. Make sure it is something that really interests you.

Hint: It is sometimes easier to approach this step by thinking of a question. For example, Why do flamingos stand on such tall, skinny legs? or Why do we have seasons such as summer and winter? or How do owls see so well at night?

Step 3:   Do some research on your topic. Find out the real, scientific reason behind why the chosen topic happens (example: thunder) or what purpose it serves (example: owl's good eyesight). Ask an adult to help you search on the Internet for information.

Hint: A good search engine to use is *www.google.com*

Step 4:   Read the information you located and take some notes on what you learn from it.

Hint: You might want to focus on some of the key words that explain your topic and other interesting facts because you can use these in your own myth.

Starting to Write:

Step 5:   Decide who the main character of your myth will be and write down some details about him or her to provide your readers with some imagery. Ask yourself some of the following questions to help you describe the main character. Write your answers on the lines provided.

Describe your character if he or she had or was a...

• Color (yellow, red, green, etc.) _____

• Feeling (happy, sad, shy, etc.) _____

• Weather condition (hurricane, sunny, freezing) _____

• Special feature (soft fur, crackled skin) _____

• Sound (blaring horn, gentle hum, whistle) _____

Remember to use these details when describing the things your character says and does!

Repeat what you did for Step 5, but this time, focus on details that will help you provide readers imagery about your setting.

Describe your setting if it was a...

• Texture (soft, cozy, rough, hard) _____

• A size (gigantic, endless, tiny) _____

• A sight (bright, dull, colorful) _____

Remember to use these details when describing your setting!

Step 6:   Write a synonym on the lines next to each of the words you chose to describe your main character and setting. Use an online thesaurus if you need help thinking of synonyms.

Step 7:   Use the graphic organizer to arrange the events of your story.

Standard W.5.6

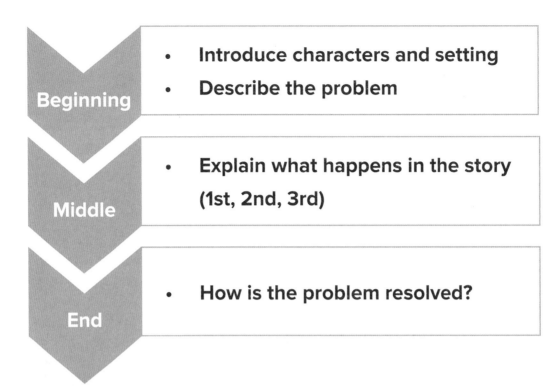

Beginning
- **Introduce characters and setting**
- **Describe the problem**

Middle
- **Explain what happens in the story (1st, 2nd, 3rd)**

End
- **How is the problem resolved?**

Transition words and phrases you might choose to use:

first   also   next   although   however   finally

Remember to use a comma after transition words that begin sentences!

Step 8: Take the information from your graphic organizer and write out your narrative using complete sentences. Be sure to include transition words and phrases to link your ideas!

Step 9: Ask an adult to read what you have written. Work together to do the following:

- Make sure you have presented your ideas clearly.
- Look for places where you can make better word choices.
- Proofread your paper for errors in grammar and mechanics.

Step 10: With the help of an adult, search online for a writing contest or creative writing magazine to which you could submit your original myth. One good place you might look is *Stone Soup Magazine*, which publishes creative writing by kids ages 8 to 13. You can find information about submitting your myth at the following link: *www.stonesoup.com/stone-soup-contributor-guideline/#general*

Poetry

Poetry is a type of writing in which the writer, or poet, carefully chooses and arranges words to create meaning, sound, and rhythm. The poet usually writes about common, everyday things but examines them in a unique way. Poetry often rhymes and is arranged in sections called stanzas. Usually, poetry contains a lot of figurative language. In this section, you will learn about different styles of poetry, types of figurative language, and point of view. You will also answer questions about the themes and meanings of poems.

Snow-flakes

by Henry Wadsworth Longfellow

Out of the **bosom** of the Air,
    Out of the cloud-folds of her garments shaken,
Over the woodlands brown and bare,
    Over the harvest-fields forsaken,
      Silent, and soft, and slow
      Descends the snow.

Even as our cloudy fancies take
    Suddenly shape in some **divine** expression,
Even as the troubled heart doth make
    In the white **countenance** confession,
      The troubled sky **reveals**
      The grief it feels.

This is the poem of the air,
    Slowly in silent syllables recorded;
This is the secret of **despair**,
    Long in its cloudy bosom **hoarded**,
Now whispered and revealed
To wood and field.

glossary

Bosom: A person's chest, where secret thoughts and feelings are kept

Countenance: A person's face or facial expression

Despair: The complete loss of hope

Divine: Excellent, delightful

Hoarded: To have accumulated or gathered a supply of something

Reveals: To show or make something known

After reading the poem "Snow-flakes," answer the questions below.

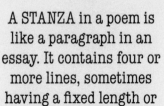

A STANZA in a poem is like a paragraph in an essay. It contains four or more lines, sometimes having a fixed length or rhyme scheme, creating a division within the poem.

1. How many stanzas or verses does the poem have? _____

2. Look at the first words in each of the lines in the stanzas. What do you notice?

    _____

    _____

    _____

3. Look at the beginning of each of the lines in the stanzas. What do you notice?

    _____

    _____

    _____

4. Why do you think Longfellow positioned the lines the way he did throughout the poem? What does it remind you of?

    _____

    _____

    _____

5. What event is happening in stanza 1?

    _____

    _____

ALLITERATION

Alliteration (uh-lit-ah-ray-shun) is a form of figurative language in which speech sounds are repeated in a sequence of words that are close together.

Usually the sound is repeated two or three times. Writers use alliteration to create a mood or emphasize certain ideas.

> **Examples:**
> **P**eter **P**iper **p**icked a **p**eck of **p**ickled **p**eppers.
> Three **g**ray **g**eese in a **g**reen field **g**razing

Use "Snow-flakes" to answer the questions below.

1. Find two examples of alliteration in stanza 1. Write the words containing the alliteration on the line provided.

_____

2. Find one example of alliteration in stanza 3. Write the words containing the alliteration on the line provided.

_____

PERSONIFICATION

Personification (per-son-if-i-kay-shun) is a form of figurative language in which a writer gives an object or idea human characteristics or abilities.

> **Examples:**
> The waves licked at the beach as the tide rolled in. (Waves can't really lick!) The rose bush stood proudly watching over the garden (Rose bushes can't really feel pride and don't have eyes to watch anything!)

1. Find an example of personification in stanza 1. Write the lines from the poem and explain how it is an example of personification.

_____

_____

2. Find an example of personification in stanza 2. Write the lines from the poem and explain how it is an example of personification. Remember to use quotation marks with any text you take directly from the poem.

_____

Spring Storm

by Jim Wayne Miller

He comes gusting out of the house,
the screen door a thunderclap behind him.   2

He moves like a black cloud
over the lawn and—stops.   4

A hand in his mind grabs
a purple crayon of anger   6
and messes the clean sky.

He sits on the steps, his eye drawing   8
a mustache on the face in the tree.

As his weather clears,   10
his rage dripping away,

wisecracks and wonderment   12
spring up like dandelions.

DETERMINING THEMES

After reading the poem "Spring Storm" by Jim Wayne Miller, answer the following questions.

1. What statement **best** reflects the main conflict, or problem, of the poem? Circle the letter of the best answer.

   A. A boy colors with a purple crayon.

   B. A thunderstorm is coming.

   C. A strong wind is gusting outside.

   D. A boy is expressing his anger.

2. Write several sentences that explain what happened in the poem.

   _____

   _____

   _____

   _____

   _____

   _____

3. How did the character in the poem resolve the conflict or problem?

   _____

   _____

   _____

   _____

PUNCTUATING TITLES

When using the title of a written work in sentences, you must set that title apart from the text surrounding it by either using quotation marks around it or italicizing (or underlining) it.

- *Italics* or <u>Underlining</u> is used for titles of larger works—books, movies, CDs, TV shows, magazines, newspapers, plays.

- "Quotation marks" are used with titles of smaller works—chapters from books, song titles, episodes of TV shows, poems, short stories, and magazine or newspaper articles.

Hint: A good way to remember these rules is that titles of larger things get italicized or underlined, while the smaller things that fit into the larger things get quotation marks.

> Examples: A poem is a shorter work that fits into a book
> (poem = quotation marks, book = italics)
>
> A song title is a shorter work that fits into a CD
> (song = quotation marks)

Read the following sentences and determine if the titles of works are properly punctuated. Write "C" on the line if the sentence is correct. Write "I" on the line if the sentence is incorrect.

1. _____   I just read the poem "Spring Storm" in my reading class textbook.

2. _____   Ben said he really enjoyed the novel "Charlotte's Web."

3. _____   My mom loves the Beatles' song called All You Need is Love.

4. _____   Miguel and I went to see the movie Batman in the theater last week.

5. _____   The headline in "The New York Times" newspaper said that my favorite novel is on the best-sellers list!

6. _____   "John Henry: The Steel Driving Man" is a tall tale based on a true story.

7. _____   Mrs. Johnson said that we will read the novel Shiloh in the spring for English class.

SIMILES AND METAPHORS

Use "Spring Storm" to answer the following questions:

1. There are two similes in this poem. Find each simile, and write them on the lines provided. Then explain what each simile is comparing.

   Simile 1: _____

   Compares _____ to _____

   Simile 2: _____

   Compares _____ to _____

2. This poem is considered an extended metaphor. In other words, the entire poem is comparing two things. Explain what two things are being compared.

   Poem compares _____ to _____

3. How did you come to the conclusion that the poem compares these two things? Provide two examples or quote two lines from the poem that explain the answer you gave in question 2. Write your answers on the lines provided.

   A. _____

   _____

   B. _____

   _____

Summer in the South

by Paul Laurence Dunbar

The Oriole sings in the greening grove
   As if he were half-way waiting,   2
   The rosebuds peep from their hoods of green,
   Timid, and hesitating.   4
The rain comes down in a **torrent** sweep
   And the nights smell warm and piney,   6
The garden thrives, but the tender shoots
   Are yellow-green and tiny.   8
Then a flash of sun on a waiting hill,
   Streams laugh that **erst** were quiet,   10
The sky smiles down with a dazzling blue
   And the woods run mad with riot.   12

glossary

Erst: long ago or formerly

Torrent: a large amount of water that moves very quickly in one direction

EXPAND YOUR KNOWLEDGE:

Paul Laurence Dunbar was a poet, novelist, and playwright in the late 1800s and early 1900s. He was one of the first African-American poets to gain national recognition for his work, and his poems still inspire modern-day readers and writers alike. You can learn more about Dunbar and read some of his poetry at the following website:

www.poetryfoundation.org/bio/paul-laurence-dunbar

Paul Laurence
Dunbar

American poet

10 cents U.S. postage

DETERMINING TOPICS AND THEMES

Topic: What the poem is about—the topic or subject of the poem

Theme: The idea the poet expresses about the subject or the message the poet wants readers to understand. The theme is usually not stated directly in a poem, and the reader must **infer**, or figure out, what the theme is. The reader should then be able to explain the theme in a complete sentence.

An easy way to remember that theme is about the message is to remember that the words "the message" begin with "theme" ┈┈┈> **The me**ssage.

After reading "Summer in the South" by Paul Laurence Dunbar, answer the questions below.

1. What is the topic or subject of this poem?

_____

2. What message, or theme, is the poet trying to express about the topic of this poem? Remember to express your idea in a complete sentence.

_____

_____

_____

_____

_____

POINT OF VIEW

In literature, point of view refers to the way authors and poets let readers see and hear what takes place in a story or poem. There are three main types of point of view.

First Person Point of View: The narrator or speaker takes part in the action and uses words such as *I* and *we*.

Third Person Point of View: The narrator or speaker does not take part in the action but tells the reader exactly what characters think and feel.

Objective Point of View: The narrator or speaker doesn't take part in the action and doesn't tell the reader anything about what the characters think or feel. He or she is just an observer.

1. What point of view is used in the poem "Summer in the South?" Explain how you can tell which point of view the speaker used. Write your answer on the lines provided.

_____

_____

_____

_____

_____

_____

_____

_____

_____

_____

_____

_____

_____

_____

FIGURATIVE LANGUAGE

Imagery–A form of figurative language that refers to the words and phrases that appeal to the senses (sight, sound, taste, touch, and smell).

> Example: One salty tear slid quietly down her rosy cheek.

Personification–A form of figurative language in which an object or idea is given human characteristics or abilities.

> Example: The days crawled by slowly.
> (Days can't really crawl on their hands and knees!)

Use "Summer in the South" to complete the activities below.

1. Find two instances of personification in the poem. Explain what is being personified, what line it appears on in the poem, and how or why this is an example of personification.

Item Being Personified	From Line #	Explanation

2. Fill out the chart below with examples of imagery from the poem that appeal to the senses. Use quotation marks around your answers.

Sight	
Sound	
Smell	

Nothing Gold Can Stay

by Robert Frost

Nature's first green is gold,

Her hardest **hue** to hold.　　2

Her early leaf's a flower;

But only so an hour.　　4

Then leaf subsides to leaf.

So Eden sank to grief,　　6

So dawn goes down today.

Nothing gold can stay.　　8

glossary

Hue: color

After reading "Nothing Gold Can Stay," answer the questions below.

1. What is the topic of this poem? How do you know?

_____

_____

2. Which of the following statements best reflects the theme of the poem?

    A. All that is certain in life is that change will come.

    B. All that we see is nothing but a dream.

    C. All that glitters is not gold, so always think carefully.

    D. All work and no play is not a good thing.

POINT OF VIEW

In literature, point of view refers to the way authors and poets let readers see and hear what takes place in a story or poem.

1. Does the speaker take part in the action of the poem? _____

2. Does the speaker tell what characters are thinking and feeling? _____

3. Based on your answers to questions 1 and 2, what is the point of view of the poem?

_____

Digging Deeper

Robert Frost was an American poet who lived from 1874 to 1963. He won four Pulitzer Prizes for poetry and many other awards for his writing. He even read one of his poems, "The Gift Outright," at the inauguration of President John F. Kennedy in 1961. You can listen to a recording of Frost reciting this poem at the following website: *www.poets.org/poetsorg/text/poetry-and-power-robert-frosts-inaugural-reading* *Scroll to near the bottom of the page to listen to the recording.*

METAPHOR, IMAGERY, AND ALLITERATION

Metaphor–Comparing two things without using the words *like* or *as*. Metaphors basically state that one thing is another.

> **Example:**   The eyes are the windows to the soul

Imagery–Words and phrases are used to appeal to the senses: (sight, sound, taste, touch, and smell.

> **Example:**   One salty tear slid quietly down her rosy cheek.

Alliteration–Speech sounds, usually consonant sounds, are repeated two or three times in a sequence of words that are close together.

> **Example:**   Sally sells seashells by the sea shore.

Use "Nothing Gold Can Stay" to answer the questions below.

1. What is the metaphor in line 1? What two things are being compared? Explain why you think the speaker compared these two things.

   _____

   _____

2. List two examples of visual (sight) imagery in the poem.

   Example 1: _____ from line _____

   Example 2: _____ from line _____

3. Fill out the table by listing two examples of alliteration and the lines in which they can be found in the poem.

Alliteration Example	Found on Line #

Standard RL.5.1, L.5.5.a, RL.5.4

Think about the changing of the seasons. Write a short essay that explains which season you enjoy the most and why. If you live in an area that does not experience changes in seasons, you can either write about what you enjoy about the year-round season you experience or write about why you like or dislike the lack of change. Use the graphic organizer to help you state your opinion and organize your reasons. Remember to use transitions, or linking words, between your points!

Introduction (State your opinion):

Reason 1: Example:	Linking Word _____ **Reason 2:** Example:
Linking Word _____ **Reason 3:** Example:	**Conclusion** (Restate your opinion):

Congratulations! You have completed the lessons in this section. Now you will have the chance to practice some of the skills you just learned.

Dreams

by Langston Hughes

Hold fast to dreams
For if dreams die   2
Life is a broken-winged bird
That cannot fly.   4

Hold fast to dreams
For when dreams go   6
Life is a **barren** field
Frozen with snow.   8

glossary

Barren: unable to produce

Activity 1

1. What form of punctuation should be used around the title of a poem used in a sentence? Fill the name of the poem you just read into the sentence below and punctuate it correctly.

    I just read the poem _____ by Langston Hughes, and I really like it.

Activity 2

1. There are two instances of alliteration in this poem. Locate them and write them on the lines below.

    _____

    _____

2. Hughes uses two metaphors in this poem. List the metaphors below and explain what the metaphors compare.

    A. _____

       Compares _____ to _____

    B. _____

       Compares _____ to _____

3. Hughes uses imagery in this poem. To which of the senses does it appeal? Circle the letter of the best answer.

    A. Smell

    B. Sight

    C. Hearing

    D. Touch

UNDERSTAND

Activity 1

Use "Dreams" to answer the questions below.

1. Does the poem rhyme at all? If so, in which lines do the rhymes occur? List your answer below.

   _____

2. How many stanzas does the poem contain?

   _____

3. Look at what Hughes says in each stanza. How is the message in each related? Write your answer below.

   _____

   _____

Activity 2

1. Write a sentence below using specific examples from the poem that describes the two things to which the poet compares a life without dreams. Remember to use quotation marks around those examples in your answer.

   _____

   _____

2. What does "Dreams" explain or teach? Summarize the message of the poem below. Include examples from the poem in your explanation.

   _____

   _____

   _____

   _____

DISCOVER

What would you say? Let's take what you have learned and write about it!

Write Your Explanation

Have you ever had a really big dream about something you wanted to accomplish or something you want to become in life? If so, you have likely run into some obstacles or difficulties that get in the way of you accomplishing your dream. Did you give up? Hopefully not!

Gathering Information:

Step 1: Reread the poem "Dreams" by Langston Hughes.

Step 2: Choose a dream or goal of yours that you would like to explain.

Step 3: Do some research on the Internet to locate some inspiring quotes about not giving up or about the importance of dreams and goals.

   Hint: A good search engine to use is *www.google.com*

Step 4: Write down one or two of your favorite quotes that you located. You may also choose to use quotes from the poem "Dreams" by Langston Hughes.

Starting to Write:

Step 5: After you have chosen the dream or goal about which you would like to write and found some inspirational quotes, start to think about some of the problems you have or might encounter as you pursue your dream or goal. Consider the ways in which you solved or plan to solve some of those problems. Use the organizer to help you gather some of those details.

Problem	Solution
1.	1.
2.	2.
3.	3.

Step 6: Use the outline below to arrange the ideas for your explanation.

    I. Introduction: State that the essay is about your dream or goal and list the problems you have or might encounter in reaching that dream or goal.

    II. Write about the first problem you encountered or might encounter.

       A. Discuss how you solved or might solve that problem.

       B. Include one of your inspirational quotes.

    III. Write about a second problem you encountered or might encounter.

       C. Discuss how you solved or might solve that problem.

       D. Include one of your inspirational quotes.

    IV. Conclusion: Restate that the essay was about your dream and how you reached or plan to reach it. (If you have not already used an inspirational quote, you could choose to use one in the conclusion.)

Step 7: Take the information from your outline and write out your explanatory essay using complete sentences. Be sure to include transition words and phrases to link your ideas!

Transition words and phrases you might choose to use:

first   also   next   although   however   finally

*Remember to use a comma after transition words that begin sentences!

Step 8: Ask an adult to read what you have written. Work together to do the following:

- Make sure you have presented your ideas clearly.
- Look for places where you can make better word choices.
- Proofread your paper for errors in grammar and mechanics.

        Standard W.5.2, W.5.4, W.5.5

Answer Key

Reading: Foundational Skills

Unit 1–Fluency
Lesson 1–Lady Liberty

Page 13. Guided Questions: 1. The statue was first built as a birthday gift from France to the United States to celebrate America's 100th birthday; 2. The Statue of Liberty has come to symbolize the United States; 3. The Statue of Liberty serves to welcome immigrants to the United States. It is also now a tourist destination; 4. Answers will vary. Possible answer: The poem helped me understand that the Statue of Liberty welcomes immigrants from all over the world to the "golden door" of opportunity in the United States. Those who are unwanted in other countries are welcomed here.

Lesson 2–Log Canoes

Page 15. Guided Questions: 1. The Powhatans made the canoes by burning and scraping out pine and poplar logs; 2. These boats became the workboats of the Chesapeake Bay because they were inexpensive to make and the supplies to make them were readily available; 3. The Powhatans used the log canoes to navigate the Chesapeake waterways and to fish. The English colonists used the waterways to transport goods, such as oysters and tobacco; 4. The English colonists added sails to the canoes to make them faster. They also began crafting log canoes with multiple hulls to haul more goods.

Lesson 3–This Is the Pits!

Page 17. Guided Questions: 1. The pits are most famous for having the largest collection of Ice Age plant and animal fossils; 2. The thick, black substance that seeps to the surface at the pits is asphalt; 3. Scientists think weak and injured animals became trapped in the asphalt and then drew predators to the scene, who also got stuck; 4. Answers will vary. Possible answers: The only complete skull of a saber-toothed tiger in the entire world was found at the tar pits.

Lesson 4–Lua Pele

Page 19. Guided Questions: 1. The Hawaiian Islands are in the Pacific Ocean; 2. Volcanoes or volcanic eruptions made the Hawaiian Islands; 3. Hot spots are places where magma pushes through the plates in the earth's crust; 4. When a volcano is called active, it means that it still erupts.

Reading and Writing: Informational Texts

Unit 2–Making History

Lesson 1–Father of Our Country

Page 24. Finding Main Ideas and Details: Possible Answer: George Washington is considered the father of our country because he was involved in many of the events that led to our independence, and he was our very first president; 2. A

Page 25. Finding Main Ideas and Details: 3. C; 4. Possible Answer: Betsy Ross's flag, the First Continental Congress, George Washington, and the Constitution are all related because they are firsts. Betsy Ross made the first flag, the first Continental Congress is the very first meeting of our government, George Washington was our first president, and the Constitution was a new formal plan for our government; 5. The United States declared itself an independent country on July 4, 1776. "On July 4, 1776, the Continental Congress signed the Declaration of Independence. They announced that the colonies were no longer under the control of the British government."

Page 26. Using Conjunctions: 1. and – joins words, 2. yet – joins sentences (independent clauses)

Page 27. Using Conjunctions: 3. and – joins words; 4. but – joins sentences (independent clauses); 5. and – joins two clauses (independent clause to a dependent clause); Challenge: Washington and a secret group from the Continental Congress visited a Philadelphia seamstress, named Betsy Ross, and they asked her to sew the very first American flag.

Page 28. Using Correlative Conjunctions: 1. not only/but also; 2. neither/nor; 3. not only/but also; 4. either/or

Page 29. Revising Sentences: Activity 1: 1. Remove "which is a town in"; 2. Remove "who was"; 3. Remove "due to the fact that" and replace with "because"; 4. Remove "As a result of the fact that" and replace with "When"; 5. Remove "those stories" and replace with "they"; Challenge: The colonial soldiers, unlike the British, did not have uniforms, so they wore their own clothes and brought along their own food and equipment.

Page 30. Revising Sentences: Activity 2: 1. Fierce; 2. Peaceful; 3. Fanciful; 4. Enthusiastically; 5. Valiantly

Lesson 2—Unfurling a Legend

Page 33. Finding Main Ideas and Details: 1.Betsy Ross sewed the first colonial American flag. There is a debate on whether or not she really made the first American flag; 2. Possible answer: Surprisingly, Ross did not become famous for making the first American flag until many years later. Not long after this visit, Ross completed the sewing of the first flag. Some historians question whether the story told by Ross's grandson is true because there are no written records about the first flag. Yet, others believe the first flag was, indeed, made by Ross for a number of reasons; Relationships Between Individuals in the Text: Possible answer: George Washington and the First Continental Congress asked Betsy Ross to make the first colonial American flag.

Page 34. Comparing and Contrasting Texts: 1. Nonfiction — it provides facts and details about a real person (George Washington) and events from history; 2. Nonfiction — it provides facts and details about a real person (Betsy Ross) and events from history; 3. The passages are both mainly structured in chronological order. The dates tell us that it is structured in the order in which the events took place; 4. The sentences from both articles have the same text structure, which is cause and effect.

Page 35. Understanding Introductory Elements: In order to earn money during the war; 2. Well known in Philadelphia for her beautiful sewing work; 3. Showing the men how to make a perfect five point star with one snip of the scissors; 4. After the war; 5. Representing each of the colonies

Page 36. Understanding Items in a Series: 1. The three men on the secret committee were George Washington, Robert Morris, and George Ross; 2. The flag had a field of blue, thirteen white stars, and thirteen alternating red and white stripes; 3. Many upholsterers took work making tents, uniforms, or flags during wartime to make money; 4. Neither Betsy, her children, nor her grandchildren realized she would become an American legend for simply sewing a flag; 5. Betsy Ross learned how to sew mattresses, chair covers, and window blinds.

Unit 3—Taking Flight!

Lesson 1—In the Clouds

Page 42. Finding Main Ideas and Details: 1. C; 2. D; 3. C; 4. D

Page 43. 5. "Charles was the first pilot to fly nonstop between New York and Paris." 6. Exemplar: The other pilots who had attempted and failed to make the transatlantic flight had multiple engine planes and copilots while Charles Lindbergh only had a single engine plane and was flying all by himself.

Page 44. Understanding Vocabulary: 1. Aviation - (noun) the art or science of flying aircraft, 2. A wing walker is a person who walks or moves on the wings of an aircraft during flight. Wing walking was common in air shows during the 1920s; Recognizing Synonyms: 1. Triumph, 2. Informed, 3. Unassisted, 4. Further, 5. Revolutionary

Lesson 2—Soaring to the Skies

Page 47. Finding Main Ideas and Details: 1. A, 2, C, 3, D, 4. B

Page 48. Finding Main Ideas and Details: 5. "Amelia Earhart became the very first female pilot to fly across the Atlantic Ocean in May of 1932." 6. Exemplar: The trip that Amelia Earhart took as a passenger on a flight across the Atlantic Ocean in 1928 made her want to try to make the flight herself.

Page 49. Using Reference Material: 1. The Distinguished Flying Cross award is a military decoration awarded to a person who is outstanding in heroism or extraordinary achievement in aerial flight, 2. Transatlantic – (adj) crossing or reaching across the Atlantic; Recognizing Antonyms: 1. Typical, 2. Demolish, 3. Undetermined, 4. Overlooked, 5. Disconnected

Unit 4—Helping People

Lesson 1—A Fearless Leader

Page 55. 1. Finding Main Ideas and Details: Susan B. Anthony helped with the antislavery movement. Susan B. Anthony was involved in education reform. Susan B. Anthony worked for women's right to vote; 2. C; Identifying Reasons and Support: Reason 1: She was an abolitionist (against slavery), Reason 2: She helped reform education. Reason 3: She fought for women's right to vote; 4. Answers will vary but may include the following responses: Evidence to support reason 1: Anthony family hosted antislavery meetings on their farm; Anthony became a member of the Anti-slavery Society in 1856; Anthony helped form a Women's National Loyal League to petition for the outlawing of slavery with the Thirteenth Amendment; Anthony fought for full citizenship and voting rights for African-Americans; Evidence to support reason 2: Anthony became involved in the teacher's union when she discovered pay differences between men and women; Anthony spoke at a state teachers' convention about pay rates and women entering all professions; Anthony urged public schools and colleges to admit women and ex-slaves; University of Rochester admitted women for the first time because of Anthony's work; Evidence to support reason 3: Anthony gave speeches and set up women's rights organizations; Anthony illegally voted in the 1872 election; Anthony had a constitutional amendment on women's right to vote introduced to Congress; Anthony appeared before Congress every year to persuade them to pass a suffrage amendment.

Page 56. Using Conjunctions: 1. After the Anthony family moved to Rochester; 2. before becoming a female principal; 3. Even though Anthony spent the majority of her life fighting for women's right to vote; 4. because of the efforts by people like Susan B. Anthony; 5. Until 1920; Activity 2: Possible answers: Susan B. Anthony went to jail because she voted in the 1872 election.

Page 57. Using Context Clues and Reference Materials: 1. Suffrage means, "the right to vote in political elections"; 2. The abolitionist movement was a movement to abolish or end slavery and set the slaves free; Revising Sentences: Questions 1-4, answers will vary. Some possible answers are as follows: 1. Susan B. Anthony voted in the 1872 election and was arrested; 2. Susan B. Anthony was very active in the abolitionist movement and dealt with angry mobs when she arranged antislavery meetings; 3. Susan B. Anthony worked as a teacher and as a head mistress at Canajoharie Academy; 4. The Susan B. Anthony coin was first made in 1979 to honor her work in the struggle for women's equality.

Lesson 2—The Conductor

Page 60. Finding Main ideas and Details: 1. Tubman worked on the Underground Railroad to free slaves. Tubman worked for the Union Army during the Civil War. Tubman worked as a nurse during and after the war to care for the sick and elderly; 2. B; Using Reasons and Evidence: Reason 1: She helped free slaves; Reason 2: She worked for the Union Army; Reason 3: She worked as a nurse to care for others; 2. Answers will vary but may include the following responses: Evidence to support reason 1: Tubman saved family members, Tubman made 19 trips and freed about 300 people, Tubman used many clever techniques to free slaves, and there was a $40,000 reward in the South for the capture of Tubman; Evidence to support reason 2: Tubman helped the Union Army with her knowledge of routes in the South, Tubman dressed as an old woman and spied in Confederate towns, Tubman assisted in a gunboat raid in South Carolina; Evidence to support reason 3: Tubman worked as a nurse during the war, using a lot of folk and

herbal remedies. Tubman created the Home for Aged to care for old people.

Page 61. Comparing Structure: 1. D; 2. Answers will vary. Possible response: Some of the key words that helped me understand both passages were dates and transition words such as in addition, first, after, later, and finally; 3. Answers will vary, but flow charts may contain some of the following things:

"A Fearless Leader": Became involved in abolitionist movement, became female principal and worked for changes in education, worked for women's rights, voted illegally and went to jail, appeared before Congress for women's right to vote; "The Conductor": Escaped slavery, helped others escape on Underground Railroad, spied for the union, worked as a nurse, created the Home for the Aged

Page 62. Using Reference Materials: The Mason-Dixon line is the boundary between Maryland and Pennsylvania. It was the northern limit of the slave-owning states before the abolition of slavery. Originally, this line was established by Charles Mason and Jeremiah Dixon in the 1700s to solve a border dispute between the colonies of Maryland and Pennsylvania; Relationships Between Words — Synonyms: 1. Witty; 2. Noted; 3. Medicine; 4. Admired; 5. Gave; 6. Old

Stop and Think! Units 1–4 Review

Page 65. Activity 1: 1. but–joins two independent clauses (i.e., a compound sentence); 2. and–joins two phrases; 3. but–joins two independent clauses (i.e., a compound sentence); 4. so-joins independent clause; Activity 2: 1. Overlooking; 2. Uncertain; 3. Harming; 4. Keeping

Stop and Think! Units 1–4 Understand

Page 66. 1. The main idea is the disagreement over whether Presidents' Day should honor Washington, Washington and Lincoln, or all past presidents; 2. Many people think the holiday should celebrate all past presidents, including Lincoln. Others think the holiday should only honor Washington because he was the first president; 3. "They say shifting the focus away from Washington would mean future generations of kids would not know about the Father of Our Country."

Pages 67. 4. The Uniform Monday Holiday Act shifted several holidays to Mondays. The change would create more three-day weekends to allow workers to spend more time with their families. It also combines George Washington and Abraham Lincoln's birthdays; 5. Something is official when it is authorized or issued by someone who holds the authority to do so; 6. Answers will vary but may include the following response: I received an official award from the principal because I made the honor roll.

Unit 5—Our Land

Lesson 1—Extreme Conditions

Page 74. Explaining Relationships: 1. Answers will vary. Possible answer: The national parks are important to the Mojave Desert region because they generate tourism and are good for the economy; 2. Preserving the Mojave is important to species such as the Joshua Tree and the Mojave Ground Squirrel because this is the only place on earth where they live. Quoting from the Text: 3. Answers will vary. Possible answer: The Mojave Desert is important to people because, "Some mining, including the mining of silver, tungsten, and iron, still takes place in the region and is an important industry."

Page 75. Explaining Reasons and Evidence: Main idea of the passage and the author's opinion is that the Mojave desert should be preserved; Evidence/reasons: Possible answers: The Mojave Desert contains unique land features. The Mojave desert is home to a species of plants and animals that are only found living there. The Mojave Desert supports tourism and mining, which are important industries in the area.

Page 76. Understanding Homographs: 1. B; 2. A; 3. B; 4. A; 5. A; 6. B; 7. A; 8. B; 9. B; 10. A

Page 77. Understanding Prefixes and Suffixes: audience-a, automatically-b, geologist-c, photograph-d, semicircle-e

Lesson 2—National Treasure

Page 80. Explaining Relationships: 1. Possible answer: It improves the quality of the water for people who live in Southern Florida because the wetlands filter the pollutants out of the water. In addition the wetlands trap overflowing water, which prevents flooding in the area; 2. Possible answer: The Everglades provide food for the manatee. Manatees and sea turtles live in the Florida Bay and feed on the special grasses that grow where the water of the Everglades meets the water of the ocean. Making Inferences: Possible answer: They would become extinct since there are only eighty to 100 Florida panthers left in the world and they reside in the Everglades.

Page 81. Explaining Reasons and Evidence: The main idea of the passage is that the Everglades is important for animals and people. This is the author's opinion. Reasons: (Possible answers) The Everglades provides a home for many endangered species. The Everglades provides clean water for people and their crops. The Everglades removes pollutants from water. The Everglades provides a place for recreation. The Everglades creates a unique environment for specific plants and animals to live.

Page 82. Using Prefixes: Activity 1: 1. Restore; 2. Interdependent; 3. React, Interact; 4. Recreation; 5. Coexist; 6. Replay; Activity 2: 1. Reduce; 2. Coexist; 3. Recreation; 4. Interdependent; 5. Restore; 6. Interact

Unit 6—Our Oceans

Lesson 1—Streaming

Page 87. Explaining Relationships: Activity 1: 1. The heat from the water in the Gulf Stream affects the climates of the areas close to it, and far away from it. Great Britain, northern Europe, and some areas in the United States have milder weather because of the Gulf Stream; 2. Possible answer: The Gulf Stream affects marine life because its eddies contain warm water where fish thrive, and turbulence from the Gulf Stream creates areas where plankton grows, which feeds fish. Quoting from the Text: Possible answer: The Gulf Stream is important to people because "The Gulf Stream has a large impact on human life. It changes our weather, and it creates areas for good fishing."

Page 88. Tag Questions: 1. The Gulf Stream affects the climate, doesn't it? 2. The Gulf Stream isn't in the Pacific Ocean, is it? 3. Small fish will be attracted to the plankton, won't they? 4. Eddies contain warmer water than what surrounds them, don't they? 5. Seamounts are things that block the flow of the Gulf Stream, aren't they? Commas with Direct Addresses: 1. Captain Smith, will the fishing be good along the Gulf Stream? 2. The Gulf Stream has an impact on climate, Don; 3. The trade winds, Maria, are what create the Gulf Stream; 4. Did you know, John, that the Gulf Stream is around 50 miles wide? 5. Aunt Sandra, I learned that the water in the Gulf Stream affects marine life.

Page 89. Verb Tense: Activity 1: 1. Blow; 2. Fed; 3. Correct; 4. Brings; 5. Correct *because these two events happen in two different time frames; Activity 2: Words from the paragraph that should be circled: pushed, created, made

Lesson 2—Saving the Sea Turtles

Page 92. Identifying Reasons and Support: 1. Sea turtles are endangered because of the threats they face, but there are ongoing efforts to save them; 2. B;, 3. D; 4. This piece of evidence shows one thing that organizations are doing to improve conditions for sea turtles.

Page 93. Revising Sentences: Answers may vary. Possible responses: 1. Sea turtles are ancient reptiles that live in all of the world's oceans; 2. People use various parts of the turtle to make and sell products, such as jewelry, that are illegal; 3. Plastic product waste washes out to sea in storm drains and rivers and harms turtles that mistake plastic items for food; 4. Scientists tag sea turtles so their feeding and nesting can be tracked with satellites, which will help scientsts decide where to create protected areas.

Lesson 3—The Life Cycle of a Sea Turtle

Page 95. Comparing Structure: 1. Possible answer: "The Life Cycle of a Sea Turtle," is compare and contrast. Sea turtles are being compared to land turtles. Similarity: Like land turtles, a sea turtle's body is protected with an upper shell called a carapace. Difference: Sea turtles cannot hide their heads and legs inside this shell like land turtles. Information From Various Sources: 1. "The Life Cycle of a Sea Turtle"; 2. "Saving the Sea Turtles"; 3. Possible Answer: Reduce the amount of artificial light that is visible from nesting beaches is the first step to reducing light pollution that affects sea turtles.

Page 96. Gathering Information From Multiple Texts: 1. Answers will vary: The sea turtle will return to the same beach where she was born to lay her eggs; 2. Possible response: Sea turtles nest on beaches, sea turtles face threats from predators and human activity, sea turtles are endangered; 3. Possible Response: "Saving the Sea Turtles" mentioned the specific threats that sea turtles face as a result of human activity and also the specific efforts that are being made to save sea turtles. "The Life Cycle of a Sea Turtle" did not discuss these details; 4. Timeline sample below:

Hatching: artificial lights

Adult: fishing threats, pollution threats, loss of nesting habitat

Juvenile: fishing threats

Unit 7—Our Skies

Lesson 1—Just Floating Around

Page 101. Drawing Conclusions and Summarizing: 1. One main idea of the passage is that there are four ways clouds form: surface heating and cooling, mountains and other high terrain, air masses being forced to rise, and weather fronts. The second main idea of the passage is that there are three general types of clouds: high, low, and middle; 2. A; 3. Possible answer: Nimbostratus clouds are low, long and streaky rain clouds. Where there are nimbostratus clouds, it is probably a gray, dreary day and either raining or snowing. "These clouds block the sun and bring rain, snow, and wind."

Page 102. Determining Meanings: Activity 1: 1. D; 2. A; Activity 2: 3. A cirrostratus cloud is a high, layered cloud;

4. An altocumulus cloud is a middle, heaped, or puffy cloud. Understanding Vocabulary: 1. The term atmosphere means the air surrounding the earth (or other planet); 2. The term terrain refers to a stretch of land, including its physical features.

Lesson 2—Northern Lights

Page 105. Summarizing the Text: 1. Answers/summaries will vary. Possible response: The Northern Lights are caused by particles from the sun carried on the solar wind entering the earth's magnetic atmosphere near the poles. This action, which happens 50 to 200 miles above Earth's surface, causes the sky to light up in beautiful patterns and colors. The Northern Lights are best viewed in places close to the north pole and are most impressive from December to March every year.

Page 106. Verb Tense: *Answers for the future perfect tense will vary based on the auxiliary used. 1. Present perfect: Some charged particles have escaped the sun's atmosphere. Past perfect: Some charged particles had escaped the sun's atmosphere. Future perfect: Some charged particles must have escaped the sun's atmosphere; 2. Present perfect: It has taken these particles 40 hours to go from the earth to the sun. Past perfect: It had taken these particles 40 hours to go from the earth to the sun. Future perfect: It ought to have taken these particles 40 hours to go from the earth to the sun; 3. Present perfect: The solar particles have torn through the earth's magnetic field. Past perfect: The solar particles had torn through the earth's magnetic field. Future perfect: The solar particles will have torn through the earth's magnetic field.

Stop and Think! Units 5–7 Review

Page 110. (Answers will vary) 1. Possible Response: Falling stars are really rocks and dust that burn up after they enter Earth's atmosphere and make streaks of bright lights in the sky; 2. Possible Response: A meteor that is big enough and does not burn completely before landing on Earth is called a meteorite. About 38,000 Meteorites have been found, mostly in the desert or in Antarctica; 3. Possible Response: When Earth passes through the trails of gas and dust left behind by comets, it causes meteor showers. As many as 100 shooting stars per hour can be seen during meteor showers.

Page 111. Verb Tense Consistency: Activity 1: 1. I (Change verb called to call); 2. I (Change verb caused to causes); 3. C; 4. I (Change verb are to were); 5. C (There is a shift, but the actions in the sentence occur at different times); Activity 2: Underline sentences 1 and 3 because they are incorrect shifts in verb tense; Sentence 2: Change verb told to tell; Sentence 4: Change verb landed to land or have landed.

Stop and Think! Units 5–7 Understand

Page 112. 1. Orbit means to travel around something in a curved path; 2. You can infer from the passage that since comets orbit the sun, the earth will pass the same comets repeatedly on a schedule; 3. "There are many comets that orbit our sun, so there are predictable times during the year when you can watch meteor showers." 4. Astronomer refers to one who studies objects and matter outside the earth's atmosphere; 5. Astronomers are scientists who study the stars and keep track of their scientific data; 6. "If you want to be like a real astronomer, count the shooting stars and record your results."

Reading and Writing: Literature

Unit 8–Tall Tales

Lesson 1–John Henry: The Steel-Driving Man

Page 121. Determining Themes: 1. B; 2. B; 3. Answers will vary. Possible response: "He had a steam-powered drill and claimed it could out-drill any man. Well, they set up a contest then and there between John Henry and that there drill."

Page 122. Hyperbole 1. Answers will vary. Possible response: Whenever words like thousands or millions are used, it is usually an exaggeration. There were probably many who lost their lives to build this tunnel, but I doubt it was thousands; 2. Answers will vary. Possible response: The story says that John Henry usually dug a total of 10 to 12 feet in one day, so it seems like a huge exaggeration that he could dig 14 feet in 35 minutes! Challenge: Answers will vary in this hyperbole activity. On the night John Henry was born, lightning struck the stars in the sky and thunder rumbled and shook the whole Earth. Just after he was born, John Henry was hungry and asked his mother for a steak and potatoes. When he did not get enough to eat, he got angry and threw the chair out of the window. After that, everyone knew not to mess around when Baby John was hungry!

Page 123. Analyzing Media: 1. Possible response: I now have a better idea what steel driving is and how hard John Henry must have worked to beat the steam drill; 2. Possible response: I learned more about how poorly the workers who built the C & O railroad and the Big Bend tunnel were treated. This makes me understand the theme of the story better.

Lesson 2–Pecos Bill Rides a Tornado

Page 125. Drawing Conclusions: 1. Answers will vary. Possible responses: Pecos Bill is famous among all cowboys; Pecos Bill was very strong and powerful; 2. Answers will vary based on question 1. Possible responses: "Now everyone in the West knows that Pecos Bill could ride anything," "Well, Bill jest grabbed that there tornado, pushed it to the ground and jumped on its back."

Page 126. Understanding Verbs: Activity 1: 1. Past progressive; 2. Future progressive; 3. Present progressive; Activity 2: Answers will vary. Possible responses: 1. I was watching the rodeo clowns perform when my sister bought me cotton candy; 2. I am watching the calf roping competition with my best friend; 3. I will be watching the rodeo competition with great interest.

Page 127. Comparing Varieties of English Dialects: Answers in this section will vary. Possible responses: 1. I think the narrator might come from the Wild West; 2. I think the author used that dialect to make the story seem more authentic and convincing, since Pecos Bill was a story cowboys would have told to each other; 3. (a) "Yep, it was that time he was up Kansas way and decided to ride him a tornado." Yes, that was the time he was in Kansas and decided to ride a tornado; (b) "Now Bill wasn't gonna ride jest any tornado, no ma'am." Bill wasn't going to ride just any tornado.

Lesson 3–Tales of Paul Bunyan

Page 129. Determining Themes: 1. The challenge in the story is that the main character, baby Paul Bunyan, is disrupting life for the citizens of Bangor, Maine; 2. To solve the problem, Paul's parents move to Minnesota where Paul will have more room; 3. Answers will vary. Possible response: Paul Bunyan was a very large baby, and his actions caused a lot of problems for the people in his town. His parents moved to Minnesota where Paul would have more room and got him a blue ox for a playmate. Paul and his blue ox, Babe, grew up and had many interesting adventures, some of which created landmarks we all know, such as the Grand Canyon.

Page 130. Learning Similes: 1. The way Paul rolls over in his sleep is being compared to a tree snapping like a twig; 2. Paul's alarm clock is being compared to a cannon; 3. Paul's stomach growling is being compared to thunder; 4. Paul's cries are being compared to train whistles; Understanding Idioms: Answers will vary. Possible responses: "took the bull by the horns" means stepping up to a challenge; "neck of the woods" means in one's own area; "elbow room" means having enough room to stretch out; "paying an arm and a leg" means paying a lot; "few and far between" means not very many.

Page 131. Challenge: Answers will vary. Possible responses: Life is like a box of chocolates; You are as strong as an ox; It fits like a glove; Revising Sentences: Answers will vary. Possible responses: Paul Bunyan was as big as a house and as strong as an ox. Not only was Paul Bunyan strong, but he was like a giant. Given his size, it's a good thing that he tried to be as gentle as a lamb in the things he did. It seemed the only thing he never managed to control was his booming voice, for he was as loud as thunder all the time.

Unit 9—Myths

Lesson 1—Why the Possum's Tail Is Bare

Page 136. Determining Themes: 1. B; 2. The problem or challenge in the story centers on Possum's bragging and pride, and the negative feelings the other animals have toward him because of it. The animals resolve the problem by cutting Possum's tail hair, which is the source of his pride; 3. Answers will vary. Possible response: "But all this time, as he wound the string around, he was clipping off the hair close to the roots, and the Possum never knew it."

Page 137. Prepositions: 1. Adverb - answers when; 2. Adverb – answers where; 3. Adjective – answers which one; 4. Adverb – answers where; 5. Adverb – answers how; 6. Adverb – answers when; 7. Adverb – answers where

Lesson 2—How the Chipmunk Got Its Stripes

Page 140. Comparing and Contrasting Stories: 1. Myths try to explain how things in the world work, or came to be, and how people should treat each other; 2. The characters in both stories are animals who live in the wild; 3. "How the Chipmunk Got Its Stripes" takes place in the meadow. Why the "Possum's Tail Is Bare" takes place in the characters' homes and townhouse. Differences: In "Why the Possum's Tail Is Bare," the Possum was proud and boastful and the other animals taught him a lesson. The story teaches that it is not good to be proud and boastful. In "How the Chipmunk Got Its Stripes," the chipmunk stood up for what he believed in to improve the lives of all the animals in the forest. This story teaches to stand up for what you believe in.

Page 141. Comparing and Contrasting Stories: 4. Under the heading, "Why the Possum's Tail Is Bare,"—The Possum was proud and boastful and the other animals taught him a lesson. Under the heading, "How the Chipmunk Got Its Stripes,"—The chipmunk stood up for what he believed in to improve the lives of all the animals in the forest. It teaches you to stand up for what you believe in; Under the heading "Both"—Both stories involve characters playing tricks on one another. Both stories involve characters becoming annoyed with one another. Both stories are about how characters came to have certain physical characteristics. They teach not to be proud or boastful; 5. "Why the Possum's Tail Is Bare" contains dialogue, and "How the Chipmunk Got Its Stripes" does not.

Page 142. Interjections: 1. Gee; 2. Hooray! (and don't forget to capitalize "We"); 3. No; 4. Wow! 5. Ouch! 6. Phew; 7. Well; Challenge: Horray! I won the literature writing contest.

Page 143. Spelling: 1. desision – decision; 2. inpatient – impatient; 3. attemt – attempt; 4. quit – quite; 5. exellent – excellent; 6. patiens – patience; 7. fourth – forth; 8. furios – furious; 9. rediculous – ridiculous; 10. freinds – friends

Lesson 3—Crow Brings Daylight

Page 146. 1. Comparing and Contrasting Settings and Events: Answers will vary: Before: dark, desperate for light, covered in blanket of blackness, drab shadows; After: mountains, valleys, and rivers came alive with light; sun gleamed and sparkled on ice and snow; colors danced with brilliance; 2. C

Page 147. Imagery: Answers will vary. Possible responses: 1. Sight – the imagery makes me think of the sunrise because the light is appearing on the horizon; 2. Sight – the imagery makes me think of the sun traveling across the midday sky because the sun is a glowing ball that moves across the sky just as crow is flying across the sky with the ball trailing behind.

Stop and Think! Unit 8–9 Review

Page 149. 1. Writers add interjections to convey emotion or to show sounds; 2. Hooray! The badger has told us the sun is a male so that we can choose a perfect name! Wow! He must be so proud of himself for being so smart. Yikes! Where is he going? Aww, he thinks we are angry with him. Gee, that's too bad; 3. Afterword – Afterward, credet – credit, humbel – humble, decision – decision, destress – distress, buge – budge, convinse – convince

Stop and Think! Unit 8–9 Understand

Page 150. 1. C; 2. Answers will vary. Possible response: "At the beginning of the era of the Surem, nobody knew the name of the sun and they wanted a name for it." 3. The conflict was resolved when the badger told everyone that the sun was a male. Now they knew what kind of name to choose for the sun; 4. The story "When Badger Named the Sun" explains why badgers do not come out of their holes onto the plains and also how everyone knew to give the sun a male name.

Unit 10—Poetry

Lesson 1—Snow-flakes

Page 156. 1. The poem has three stanzas; 2. The words out, over, even, and these are repeated; 3. The second and fourth lines of each stanza are indented, and the fifth and sixth lines of each stanza are indented even farther; 4. Indenting the alternating lines imitates the way snowflakes dance back and forth as they float down from the sky. Repeating the first words in the lines makes the reader think about how many snowflakes (that look the same to the naked eye) are falling from the sky; 5. It is starting to snow.

Page 157. Alliteration: 1. brown, bare and silent, soft, slow; 2. Slowly, silent, syllables; Personification: Answers will vary. Possible responses: 1. "Out of the bosom of the air." The air does not have a chest; 2, "The troubled sky reveals / The grief it feels." The sky cannot feel sadness.

Lesson 2—Spring Storm

Page 159. Determining Themes: 1. D; 2. In the poem "Spring Storm," a boy is angry and rushes out of his house. He is so angry that he imagines taking a purple crayon and smearing it across the sky and drawing a mustache on a tree. Eventually, he calms down and gets back to normal; 3. The conflict in the poem is resolved as he sits on the porch and has some time to calm down.

Page 160. Punctuating Titles: 1. C; 2. I; 3. I; 4. C; 5. I; 6. C; 7. C

Page 161. Similes and Metaphors: 1. "He moves like a black cloud" — compares his movement to the movement of a black cloud; "Wisecracks and wonderment spring up like dandelions" — compares his wisecracks and sense of wonder to dandelions; 2. The poem compares the boy's bout of anger or temper tantrum to a spring storm; 3. Answers will vary. Possible response: "A hand in his mind grabs a purple crayon of anger and messes the clean sky." In his rage, he imagines coloring the sky purple (which is the color it turns during a bad storm); "as his weather clears, his rage dripping away" – as his weather clears, his anger starts to go away. It drips like rain.

Lesson 3—Summer in the South

Page 163. Determining Topics and Themes: 1. The topic of the poem is summer; 2. Dunbar is trying to send the message that summer in the South is beautiful!

Page 164. "Summer in the South" is told from the objective point of view. The speaker is just an observer telling us what he sees. He does not take part in the action and there are no characters.

Page 165. Personification: 1. Answers will vary. Possible responses: Rosebuds, line 3; Rosebuds are personified because they can't peep (no eyes), and they don't wear hoods (only people wear clothes); Streams, line 12; Streams are personified because streams cannot really laugh; 2. Answers will vary. Possible responses: Sight: "Then a flash of sun on a waiting hill"; Sound: "The Oriole sings in the greening grove"; Smell: "And the nights smell warm and piney"

Lesson 4—Nothing Gold Can Stay

Page 167. Determining Topics and Themes: 1. The topic of the poem is about new spring plants growing and changing; 2. A; Point of View: 1. No (just an observer); 2. No; 3. "Nothing Gold Can Stay" is told from the objective point of view.

Page 168. Metaphor, Imagery, and Alliteration: 1. "Nature's first green is gold." The first green leaves of nature are being compared to gold. Possible explanation: The speaker of the poem compares the first signs of spring (nature's first green) to gold, a valuable metal. The speaker thinks that the new leaves of spring are precious and valuable; 2. Answers will vary. Possible answers: "Nature's first green is gold" and "Then leaf subsides to leaf"; 3. Answers will vary. Possible response: "Her hardest hue to hold" (Line 2); "So dawn goes down to day" (Line 7)

Stop and Think! Unit 10 Review

Page 171. Activity 1: 1. "Dreams"; Activity 2: 1. dreams die and broken-winged bird; 2. A) "Life is a broken-winged bird/That cannot fly." – Compares life to a broken-winged bird; B) "Life is a barren field / Frozen with snow." – Compares life to a barren field. 3. B. Sight

Stop and Think! Unit 10 Understand

Page 172. Activity 1: "For if dreams die" … "That cannot fly" … "For when dreams go" … "Frozen with snow"; 2. One; 3. "Life is a broken-winged bird / That cannot fly." – Compares life to a broken-winged bird; "Life is a barren field / Frozen with snow." – Compares life to a barren field; Activity 2: The poet compares life without dreams to a bird with broken wings. He also compares life without dreams to a field with nothing – no trees or grass and it cannot produce anything. 2. This poem teaches that in order for life have true meaning, we have to have a dream—something that moves us to do great things. If we have dreams, then we will always produce good results in the different things that we do and we will work hard at becoming successful in the things we choose to do.

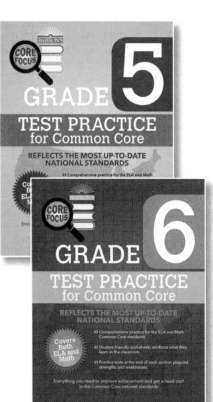

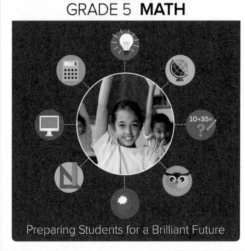